AF255485

Woodworking

2 Books in 1

The Complete Guide To Essential Woodworking Skills and Techniques to Makes Your Indoor and Outdoor Project

By

Jake Wood

The trademarks that are used are without any consent, and the publication of the trademark is without permission or backing by the trademark owner. All trademarks and brands within this book are for clarifying purposes only and are the owned by the owners themselves, not affiliated with this document.

Table of Contents

WOODWORKING FOR BEGINNERS

WOODWORKING PROJECTS

Woodworking for Beginners

The Complete Step by Step Book of Woodworking With Techniques, Skills, Tools and Tips For Create Your Projects

By

Jake Wood

Introduction

There are several directions to take when you first begin woodworking, including forks in the track, dead ends, & shortcuts. Our forefathers must embark on this quest with the assistance of a live, breathing guidance: a leader, a grandfather, or a shop instructor.

Regrettably, the number of guides has decreased in recent years. As a result, you're left to rely on people like us for assistance. It's not a beautiful picture, much like the production of meat byproducts. Learning woodworking from books, magazines, TV, & the occasional lesson is a gradual way to master a difficult skill. Many woodworkers, in particular, expend a significant amount of time (years) merely collecting machinery and equipment before building a single piece of wood equipment. And once they start building, they'll quickly find that they'll need various equipment and resources to accomplish their goals.

As a result, they increase their tool and machine purchases. We would like you to realize something that isn't always mentioned: there is a certain way to start making furniture. You won't require a workbench, table saw or even a store to complete a project. To create the first birdhouse, you do not need to invest $1,000. You will head to the home early in the morning & begin working on a project the same day. We're still not just about constructing junk. A table saw isn't the difference b/w a nice-looking collection of bookshelves & a haphazard assembly of 2x4s. Cleverness, sound design, & a little patience make all the difference. You'll need a few good tools that you won't outgrow to make comfortable furniture. This book will assist you in choosing the best resources that strike a compromise between cost and functionality. These tools must be used correctly; we'll teach you how to build furniture with them (something one can seldom see in the guidance manual). You'll need a spot to work, it may be a driveway, workshop, or a section of the basement. You'll need decent supplies, which we'll show you how to buy from your nearest home base. You'll also need designs and concepts for items to design that is both attractive and feasible to create using these technologies, processes, and materials. The plans can be found in a column that appears on any topic of Popular Woodworking.

We believe that as your abilities develop, you can outgrow this book. We're sure you'll need a table saw at some stage. There's even a drill press. There's even a plane for smoothing things out. You would, though, have a room full of well-built, well-proportioned, ventures under your belt before the day arrives. You'll be prepared with such incredible gadgets, & the learning curve would be significantly reduced. If all of this seems like something concocted by a group of idealists at a business planning conference, you're mistaken.

Chapter 1: Basics of Woodworking

Woodworking includes a wide range of practices such as woodcarving, turning, marquetry, cabinetmaking, & joinery; nevertheless, any specialist craftsman/craftswoman has perfected the fundamentals of marking and measuring, assembling, dimensioning, and finishing, which is deemed the foundations of every woodworking calling.

To trace out the wood for even a project and visualize how one part works with another & in what order is expected of a woodworker, the capacity to think in 3 directions is required. You'll also need to recognize which instruments can provide the best performance, based on the degree of precision needed and the wood's properties.

Dimensioning is the method of precisely minimizing raw materials to size accurately. This almost always necessitates planning modules square & true – a technique that is straightforward in theory but requires a great deal of experience to master.

All but the easiest woodworking designs include cutting and welding a number of joints. Joinery, which has long been viewed as a barometer of a woodworker's abilities, necessitates strong hand-eye coordination, yet practice can teach you how to join two pieces of wood in an appealing and discrete manner without compromising strength.

An understanding of how wood acts is a crucial complement to these essential skills. It's a one-of-a-kind, living material that swells and contracts in response to variations in humidity, which a woodworker must account for in the design and development of any project. Some woods are simpler to deal with than others, & each piece is different in the sense the grain bends and turns, independent of species.

There is no one-size-fits-all approach to woodworking. The correct method is the one that fits better for you, and that means striking a compromise between the time it takes, the resources accessible, the satisfaction you get from the procedure, and the consistency of the outcomes you seek.

For woodworking, there are reasons for both the usage of hand tools & the use of computers. Hand tools, according to others, help you to learn the "knack" for cutting & shaping wood without ripping the grain. Other woodworking experts argue that regardless of the setup period taken for mechanical equipment, you will always finish a project in less time using hand tools. Others, on the other hand, have the same viewpoint. In this book, we'll go through both options: hand tools & machine tools.

You don't have to be someone like Bob Villa to create anything you'll love for years with a little persistence, the right tools and strategies, and a decent collection of plans.

Chapter 2: Seven Woodworking Techniques and Strategies Everybody Should Know

In the 1880s, high schools began offering "industrial arts" classes, & for the next era, taking a lesson in woodworking, drafting, mechanics, or printing was a popular educational badge of honor for young men.

And, starting many decades back, shop lessons were phased out of high school curricula. Schools continued to eliminate electives, institute tougher graduation standards, and concentrate more on special education academics & the subjects required for passing state exams as educational resources decreased and the reliance on standardized tests increased. Since there was no funding or time to support equipment and sawdust-filled classrooms, school systems began to eliminate shop courses, assuming that students interested in trade training could study them later at a technical college.

This is a shame since shop lessons were never exclusively for the purpose of training students for trade careers. Rather, whether they want to be a carpenter or a doctor, they instructed all men particular skills which they could use & appreciate during their lives. They were seen as essential to developing a well-rounded man who could utilize both his hands & his mind.

Woodworking has evolved from a simple necessary talent to something more mystical or awe-inspiring in our era of plastic and factories. Since most 21st-century shoppers are used to heading to big-box retailers to buy another mass-produced substitute when their desk or chair fails, any man who can step up to a timber pile with a saw & plane to form a lovely and long-lasting replacement is regarded as a "real craftsman."

While there is widespread respect for hand skills, the fact is that woodworking is not a wonder. And, luckily, it's never too late to learn if you didn't take a rigorous shop course in college and felt unprepared to handle a basic woodworking project. Here's a rundown of certain fundamental skills you can work on. None of these abilities necessitate the use of costly, hazardous equipment or unusual tools. They are the fundamental abilities that any woodworker should possess.

2.1 Comprehend How Wood Works & Behaves?

Before you can use any tool on the lumber, you must first determine its proper orientation & the direction in which you can plane the board. Growth ring layers begin to expand on one another as trees rise, resulting in beautiful grain in the boards. If we neglect the best working path, this grain will make planing more challenging. Working with wood grain is similar to petting a cat: if you go from tail to head, the fur may stick straight up and you will get a hissing rejection, but if you go from head to tail "with the grain," the hairs will lie down soft & smooth & purring may ensue.

It's also crucial to know how wood spreads & contracts as humidity levels change during the year. This natural property is taken into account of all wooden architecture, and ignorance of it may be catastrophic.

2.2 Sharpen Planes, Saws, and Chisels

So many individuals have perpetuated the misconception that dealing with wood by hand is extremely difficult merely by using a boring instrument. It's a thing of faith among woodworkers that you should "let the tool do the job" if you want things to move smoothly. You aren't doing yourself any favors if the saw takes a lot of force to cut or if you require a good push to make shavings with the hand plane. Sharpening the tools is a fundamental skill and it is something that must be done on a daily basis. Working with dull equipment is not just inefficient, but often risky. If you find like you have to drive your chisel with the bodyweight to finish the break, you will lose momentum and the tool will stab through anything it comes into contact with. If you know how to sharpen the tools, you'll find that woodworking is fun, safe, & efficient.

2.3 Hand Plane Usage

The simple method is fairly self-explanatory with a number of woodworking materials. However, not each of them is as intuitive as most. To create the feel of changing the cut from rough to fine, proper usage of hand planes necessitates some training and practice. Furthermore, the edge may be crooked or the cap iron may be positioned incorrectly. While it takes a little bit of study to figure out how to use a hand plane properly, it is an undoubtedly attainable skill. Pick an old plane and go to YouTube to look up "tune-up an old hand plane" or "how to use a hand plane." There would be plenty of footage to compensate for what you lost in shop class.

2.4 Preparation of Lumber with Hand Tools

You might already have a tablesaw & a 13-inch thickness planer, but most of us don't. Make sure you don't get caught up with the idea that you have to use costly equipment to create stuff. You just have to use hand tools while working with wood, and you will enjoy every minute of it. Woodworking by hand is effective & viable if you understand how artisans employed their lumber before machinery ruled the furniture industry. There are a number of tried-&-true methods for speeding up the operation that relieves us of the burden of having to perform machine-perfect work manually. The trick is to use the appropriate tool for the task: coarse tools for doing the coarse job, fine tools for doing the fine job.

2.5 Cut a Mortise & Tenon Joint

In all wood development, this is the most basic joint. We must interlock horizontal members (such as a chair rail) with vertical members (such as a leg) at a right angle whenever we join them. We may make a stable 90° joint by putting a tenon into a subsequent mortise (hole). Although it may seem simple to produce, creating a comfortable, close fit takes meticulous technique and practice. There are a variety of ways to create a mortise, but you will like to use a sturdy chisel made for the job and clearly calculate the width of the tenon using the chisel's dimension. 4 straight saw cuts are normally used to cut the tenon. When you figure out how to better set out this joint and carve it to a tight match, the realm of woodworking expands to you. You should now be familiar with all of the joinery used to construct most tables & chairs.

2.6 Cut Dovetail Joints

What if you'd like to make a box? The cherished (and excessively confusing) dovetail joint is a powerful place to connect boards at their corners. The dovetail joint is very much awe-inspiring of all the characteristics that non-woodworkers enjoy today. It's made up of wedge-shaped "tails" on one side that fits into corresponding "pins." The wedge form stops the boards from falling apart in one dimension while they are fitted together. Since the 1700s, this joint has been a very popular design. Never intended to impress, it was frequently concealed under veneer, molding, or paint so no one had to see the "ugly" joinery. Visible joinery was not deemed an architectural commodity until the arts & crafts movement. Making dovetail joints became a litmus test for professional woodworkers in recent years, but don't let that deter you from giving it a shot. Get into the shop after seeing a couple of the 4M "How to Cut Dovetails" videos available online. It's way simpler than most people believe: Tails must be cut. On the other board, trace the tails. The waste you traced should then be cut out. That's what there is to it. All of the refinement is just a matter of practice.

2.7 Finish the Furniture

How are you aiming to finish a good table or chest after spending some weekends working on it? Finishes enhance and preserve the piece you have worked so hard to create, so don't skimp and only "rub it with oil." There are so many lovely finishes to choose from that it becomes second nature to deal with them. Shellac is used 99 percent of the time. It's very easy to apply once you get the hang of it, very forgiving, quickly repairable, & you never have to scrub a brush (since it re-softens in ethanol). Other varnishes that are suitable for outdoor usage are also accessible.

Chapter 3: Basic Tools for the Tool Shop

Woodworking involves different stuff to different folks. To alleviate tension and exercise their artistic muscles, many woodworkers make useful and long-lasting objects. They're enthusiasts who know sawdust is healthy for the spirit. Others decide to choose a career. They're well compensated for their expertise in creating sought-after furniture. Regardless of if you're a skilled craftsperson or a rank novice, you'll need the essential woodworking equipment. For more detail on these methods, read the full section. In a nutshell, the following are essential woodworking tools:

- Hand saws
- Power saws
- Sanders
- Planes
- Hammer
- Files
- Drill
- Mallet
- Tape Measure
- Square
- Screw Gun
- Workbench
- Sawhorses

The huge variety of resources commercially available can be overwhelming for new woodworkers. It's quick for you to pile up the money worth of costly woodworking equipment in your store. Most tools for novice woodworkers do not have to be detailed and expensive, however. Beginner woodworking tools should focus on the fundamentals so that you can develop the sense of ease that is at the heart of successful work.

There are 5 classes of simple woodworking tools. Those are instruments to cut, assemble, finish, measure & hold wooden pieces when converting raw materials into finished designs. These tool classes provide all a beginner woodworker would need to construct easy to complex objects. Here's a beginner's guide to must-have woodworking tools to help you priorities what can go in your basic toolbox.

3.1 Woodworking Saws

Cutting materials is the first step in almost every woodworking project. Starting with ragged lengths of wood, the best & most interesting pieces emerge. Wood stock requires ripping & crosscutting to begin taking shape, whether it's hardwood such as oak or softwood such as pine. Saws are the solution, but they come in a variety of sizes and shapes. They're also useful for a variety of cutting tasks. Here's everything you'll need to get started on your saw collection.

3.2 Jigsaw

A good jigsaw is essential for any beginner woodworker. Because of the saber-like, reciprocating, blade, they're often known as saber saws. These electric power tools are made to create delicate smooth, angled, and serpentine cuts. Consider the outlines in a jigsaw puzzle to get an idea about what a jigsaw can do.

Circular saws and jigsaws are not the same things. Jigsaws use a back-and-forth or up-and-down motion to slash rather than spinning knives. The number of teeth and the structure of blades differ. They may be used to cut metal, plastic, & wood. Sawing veneers need fine-tooth blades, whereas rough and fast operation necessitates coarse-tooth blades.

Jigsaws are simple to use with only one side. This encourages you to use the other hand to firmly hold your work. Jigsaws are excellent for cutting small, intricate pieces. Interior cuts, such as rectangle or inner circle, are one of the easiest uses for a jigsaw. Drill a pilot hole & then insert the blade. With a little practice, you'll be able to create plunge cuts with the jigsaw in no time.

3.3 Compound Miter Saw

Regular circular saws are a step down from compound miter saws. They take the same crosscut, rip, and combination blades like circular ways. They are, though, set in an arm or track, similar to radial arm saws they have completely replaced. The most popular blade diameters are 10 & 12 inches, but compound miter saws will use the smaller 7.5" scale. Often use a high-quality crosscut saw blade for a miter saw.

These electric saws are highly adaptable instruments. In most stores, they've taken the place of the traditional miter box & backsaw. Power miter saws provide much more precise cuts for miters, bevels, & compound angles, according to beginners. Standard angles like 22.5, 45, and 90 ° are simple to set, but they can be modified for any angle in between. This applies on both left & right cuts.

The traditional cut-off/chop saw gave way to powered miter saws. Versions with sliding arms which stretch cut lengths are now available. Their powerheads often tilt to one hand, allowing for miter & bevel cuts to be combined. A compound miter saw can cut almost any set of angles.

3.4 Table Saw

The majority of new woodworkers buy a table saw right away. Table saws can make cuts that are difficult to do with other forms of saws. They're made to look like upside-down rotating saws, with the blade visible from under the saw table/work surface. Precision can be achieved by adjusting the blade depth & angle.

There are three different types of table saws. All three are appropriate for novice woodworkers. It depends on how many tasks you'll be performing and when you'll be doing it. A fixed table saw which remains in one shop position or a compact table saw which can be packed away are all options. Following are the table saw options available to you:

Cabinet table saws are big and powerful, and they're built to stay put. The name derives from the fact that their motors are housed in a lower cabinet, with a belt and pulley mechanism driving the blade. They're great at anything from lumber tearing to panel cutting. A cabinet table saw is also the focal point of a beginner's workshop.

Benchtop table saws are less efficient than full-sized table saws. They're designed to be compact, so they're ideal for transporting between locations and storage while not in operation. Direct drive table saws make up the majority of benchtop table saws. This allows them to be portable, but it still makes them noisy.

The tightest designs are contractor table saws. On job sites where time and room are limited, building contractors choose them for fast and simple cutting. Contractor table saws are often cost-effective, making them a decent option for newcomers studying how to use them.

When using a table saw, also regarded as a chop saw / chop box, do use a high-quality blade, such as Luxite Saw's carbide tip combination blades / rip saw blades.

3.5 Bandsaw

When it comes to ripping rough stock or creating delicate angled slices, nothing beats a bandsaw. The teeth are mounted on a permanently looped, flat steel band & revolve through upper and lower pulleys in these power tools, which are a mixture of circular and saber saws. Between the pulleys is a flat table that leans for angled cuts.

Bandsaws are available in a variety of styles. It depends on the scale of the stock and the complexity of the cuts you choose to produce. There are two major bandsaw features to be mindful of, and each one influences the scale of your bandsaw:

The depth capacity of a bandsaw is the distance between the pulleys where the blade is exposed. It's also known as the face opening, and it ranges from 4" for tiny bandsaws to 12 inches or more for larger devices. The thickness of your content capability is determined by this.

Throat depth is measured from the back of the support structure to the blade teeth. This decides the size of your stock. Making curved cuts where work has to be turned on the table is better with a deep throat capability.

Bandsaw teeth are available in coarse and fine designs, with coarse teeth for fast cuts & fine teeth for smoother, slower cuts. For bandsaws, blade diameter is crucial. Broad blades are better for ripping, whereas narrow blades are better for angled cutting.

And sure to get a decent band saw tires for your bandsaw and get the most out of it.

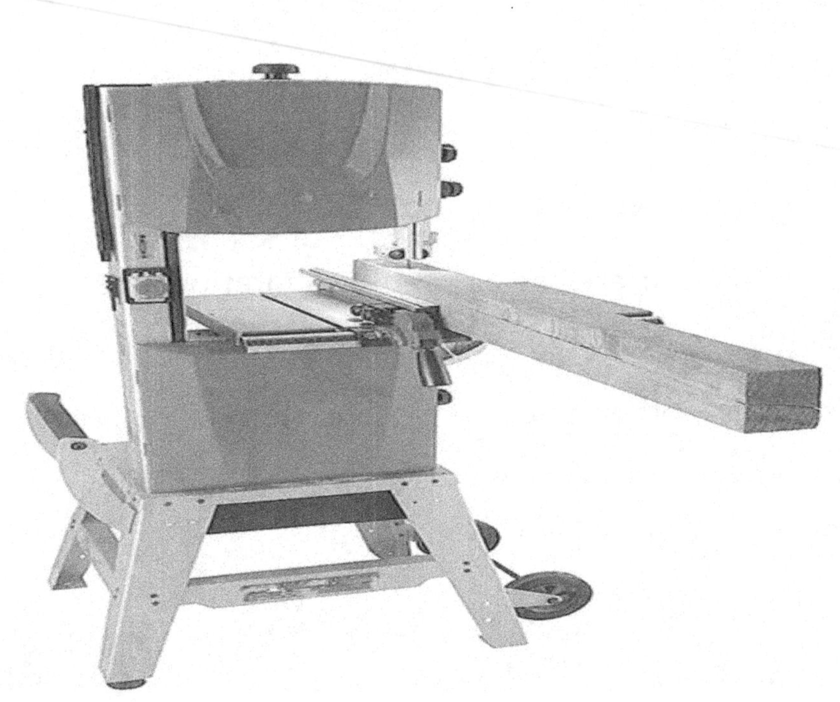

3.6 Handsaws

Handsaws will still have a spot in every woodworker's workshop. Handsaws are ideal for swift work or where precise, accurate cuts are needed. The advantage of handsaws is that they have no heavyweight, clumsy wires, or batteries. Handsaws are still available to use and are well priced.

For hundreds of years, people have used handsaws. They consist of a toothed steel blade consists of a wooden handle that slides back and forth to cut the work. But there's a lot more about using a handsaw that most people realize. Find the following handsaw designs:

Ripping Handsaws: Cut with a grain of wood.

Crosscut Handsaws: Cut into the grain of the wood.

Combination Handsaws: Can perform both rips and crosscuts.

Backsaws: Rectangular blades for miter cuts with braced backs.

Carcase Handsaws: Backsaws that are larger and stronger.

Coping Handsaws: Handsaws for curved cuts, similar to jigsaws and bandsaws

Dovetail handsaws: To make fine dovetail joints.

Keyhole handsaws: Handsaws for cutting interior holes.

Beginner woodworkers can buy the highest-quality handsaws they can. The majority of hand sawing frustrations stem from inexpensive or rusty blades. A sharp blade with good teeth can cut wood just as quickly as accurately as an electric saw.

3.7 Circular Saw

A circular saw is one of the power-activated saws that should be in every beginner's toolbox. There are a plethora of brands to choose from, but they all have one thing in common. It's a blade with sharp teeth that rips through the wood in a round or square shape. Electric circular saws are available in a variety of strength grades. The majority of circular saws are corded and operate on the household present, but cordless circular saws have made significant progress.

Circular saws are thought to be more for rugged carpentry than fine woodworking by others. That isn't the case at all. Circular saws, with the right hands, create smooth, tidy sections. The blade you use has a significant impact.

There are three varieties of circular saw blades:

Ripping Blades: Cut stuff lengthwise with or toward the grain with these blades.

Crosscut Blades: They are used to saw through the grain.

Combination blades: Blades that can be used for both ripping & crosscutting.

The arrangement of blades' teeth distinguishes them. Crosscuts have staggered teeth while ripping blades have equally spaced teeth. Both tooth layouts are present in combination blades. If money is an issue, it's better to buy a single decent combination blade with carbide teeth. It's also essential to know about blade diameters. Circular blades begin at 7.5", however, 10" and 12" diameters are required for high dimensional woodcutting.

There are two types of circular saws on the market. The blade is placed 90 ° to the motor & directly on the arbor in a direct push. The most popular and least costly circular saw is the direct drive. Circular saws with a worn drive are designed for tough employment. They have the same blade designs as before, but the blade is powered by a gear instead of the engine.

3.8 Filing, Planing, & Sanding

Once the wood parts have been cut to a rough form, they may need more work to achieve a pleasing, finished appearance. You'll need filing, planing, and sanding materials regardless of how sharp the saw blade is or how good the standard is. Here are several things that novice woodworkers may suggest purchasing:

Planes

Planes are not abrasive sanding machines, but rather cutting equipment. A fixed blade is used in all varieties of planes to shave off the wood fibers, allowing them to take form and get smoother with time. The scale and depth of the blades are the most important factors in determining how much material may be removed at one point.

You'll learn a few plane names that are unfamiliar, if not amusing. Both rabbet planes & jack planes shave wood, but they've somewhat different purposes. Jointers, blocks, & spokeshaves are all words you'll hear. You'll hear them alluded to by numbers as well. Beginning woodworkers can look at both of these different kinds of hand planes. The following is a list of hand planes that you may be interested in:

The Jack Plane: It is a tool that can clear a lot of material with one pass. Since it comes with both curved and straight edge models — for smoothing and jointing, respectively — this is a "jack-of-all-trades" product.

Block Planes: These are sturdier and smaller planes. They're great for close work that necessitates very straight joints.

Joining Planes: These planes are similar to jack planes, but they're used to smooth edges & join pieces together. Jointers typically have long frames.

Rabbet planes: They are used to carve right angle grooves down the grain of a board. These joints are known as rabbets, as opposed to dadoes, which are inside grooves.

Scraper Planes: Designed to scrape fine fibers from wood surfaces for ultra-smooth results. Cabinet scrapers are another name for these planes.

Spoke shaves: They are hand planes built for curved surfaces. Originally intended for wagon wheel spokes, they have now made their way into the hands of all woodworkers.

Sanding

Your staining project would move smoother and better if you have a basic understanding of sanding & preparing wood before staining.

Power Tools or Sandpaper

The amount of sand granules each square inch of paper determines the grit of sandpaper. The higher the amount, the higher the quality of the category. Sandpaper of a lower grade is coarser. Each sheet's grit number is usually printed on the back.

Sandpaper in medium and fine grades is often used to refinish furniture and antiques. A fine wood finish is harmed by coarse grits (grits less than #100). For removing old finishes or cracks, medium grits such as #120 & #150 are useful. Final light sanding with fine grits, like #220, is popular just before adding stain to the wood.

Though power tools help sanding move smoother, heavy-duty ones like belt sanders are made for harder carpentry work and may easily destroy a valuable antique. For refinishing, a palm sander, a streamlined rotary sander, is better.

For fine finishes & delicate pieces, hand sanding is preferred. Rip sandpaper sheets into quarters, then shape them into three-finger sections. Wrap a strip of sandpaper across a block of wood which sits in your hand to build a temporary sanding aid. Using a contoured sanding board, which you can find at hardware stores, connect sandpaper by putting the ends into grooves on each end of the block.

Sand with the Grain

When you look at a piece of wood closely, you'll see holes in the surface that create a sequence called the grain. Sand in the grain's path, never at an angle or perpendicular to it. This is often applied while performing on hard-to-reach edges and corners. Scratches created by sanding against the grain can appear unsightly in the finished product, which will be particularly visible after staining.

Place the piece so the sanding surface is horizontal & at a suitable height for you. Keep the sanding block flat and tightly apply even pressure when going back & forth through the same orientation as the grain for a smooth finish. Excessive pressure or the use of the sanding block's corners can result in unintended depressions in the wood.

When using a palm sander, the same principles apply: sand with the grain & apply even pressure when holding the sander flat against the wood.

Orbital Sander

Orbital sanders are different from inline instruments like belt sanders in that they utilize sandpaper pads that rotate in an orbital or circular pattern. If you just purchase one electric wood-finishing product, make it an orbital sander.

Regular orbital sanders rotate a revolving abrasive sandpaper disc in a loop, removing content quickly while leaving swirl markings that are difficult to erase. A random orbital sander, on the other hand, does not pulse but rather oscillates in a spontaneous fashion, making the wood substrate silky smooth & mark-free.

3.9 Hand Files

When it comes to shaping and smoothing wood, there's no finer instrument than a hand file. Hand files are cheap and last a lot longer if you choose ones crafted of high-quality steel. When hand files get rusty, it's safer to repair them rather than attempt to sharpen them.

Rasps are coarse-toothed, rough-edged instruments that are used to cut vast volumes of wood for general forming before finer files take over.

Half-round files do have a smooth one hand and a twisted one, allowing them to be used on both straight & curved surfaces.

 Mill files are smooth on all sides, with coarse teeth on one & fine teeth on the other side, and toothed edges for working in small spaces.

Rotary cutters are similar to hand files, but they're electronic drill bits that you insert into the drill chuck & let the rotary abrasive movement strip stuff. They come with a variety of patterns & cutting grits.

Hand files are often used to sharpen other woodworking blades & parts. Metal files are normally made of high-grade steel and have exceptionally fine teeth. As with any instrument, you get what you pay for, so it's worth investing in high-quality hand files.

3.10 Tools for Assembling

Cutting & smoothing wood is just part of the process; if the parts are correctly sized and clean enough for finishes, they must be assembled. Successful woodwork construction requires two things: precision joints that align, and the right tools to install and firmly fasten them.

For beginning woodworkers, these are the main assembly tools:

Hammer

There is no such thing as a standardized woodworking hammer. A carpenter's claw hammer can be the closest thing to a one-size-fits-all pounding tool, but there are hundreds of other styles. Woodworking hammers are typically asked to perform two functions: pry and pound. How well they achieve these tasks relies on a few factors:

Some heads are flat, such as those used in finishing hammers, and others have serrated faces for grasping nails and fasteners, such as those used in framing hammers.

Finishing hammers have long & pronounced claws, while framing instruments have a straighter edge used to cut objects.

Most starting woodworkers choose a wooden or plastic hammer handle because it delivers less shock when hitting. Framers choose steel handles because steel contributes weight to the handle, which increases pushing power. Steel handles often don't snap easily.

Hammer weight is calculated in ounces, with lightweight hammers weighing 8 to 10 ounces, intermediate hammers 16 to 20 ounces, and heavy-duty hammers 24 to 32 ounces.

Hammers come in a variety of shapes and sizes, as well as different materials. Beginner woodworkers have a lot of options, and they can figure out what they will be using the hammers for before buying them. The following are the most popular styles of woodworking hammers:

Finishing hammers may be used for a variety of tasks. Since they're so useful, this could be the first buy.

Framing hammers are very durable. They are, though, overkill for most woodworking ventures.

Tack hammers function similarly to brad drivers. They're designed for smaller jobs and generally come in two sizes with no claws.

Mallet

Mallets are not to be confused with hammers. Both are eye-catching gadgets, but they have very different purposes. The majority of hammers have a steel face, but others are brass or rubber. Mallets have detachable handles and wide wooden or leather heads to match a variety of head sizes.

The striking shock & surface impression of hammers and mallets are what distinguishes them. Mallets are softer than hammers which absorb rather than transmit shock. Mallets are ideal at tapping wood joints together since they leave minimal strike impressions.

Beginner woodworkers should be aware that chisels should never be hit with a steel hammer. Chisels stab or jab at the wood as a result of the shock from steel hammers, leaving rugged finishes. Chisels, on the other hand, maybe tapped with a mallet to smoothly slice into wood with constant strength.

Power Drill

A beginner woodworker's best buddy maybe a power drill. A brace & hand drill or a bit are only used by just a few old-school craftspeople. Electric drills are used often in the workshop for a variety of purposes. They're useful for more than just digging holes. You should get a variety of adapters to transform your electric drill into a variety of different gadgets.

If you're purchasing the first power drill, a corded model is a good option. Drills that operate on 110/120-volt currents provide a lot of torque and last a lot longer than cordless drills. Some may think cords are inconvenient, but they will never disappoint you with a low charge.

If you choose cordless control drills, keep in mind that they will be rated in voltage. The first versions had a 7.5-volt battery, although this was soon updated. For starters, 18-volt cordless drills have become a good option. They're not much more costly than 14-volt drills, but they're a lot stronger.

Power drills are often classified by chuck scale, with 3/8" chucks being the most typical medium-size & 1/2" chucks being the most heavy-duty. Drills come with keyed or keyless chucks, which render changing bits a convenience.

Screw Gun

Screws are the best fasteners for woodworking in general. They are secure and may be replaced for disassembly, temporary joints, or when errors occur. While you don't want to be without the normal hand screwdrivers, a powered screw gun allows turning screws quicker and easier. When you have work that requires a lot of screws, a screw gun comes in handy.

Screw guns are a subset of the power drill group of tools. The majority of screw guns are also cordless, making them more comfortable. The inside outline of the chuck is the biggest distinction between a real screw gun & a power drill. Screw guns are used to put six-sided or hexagonal bit shanks into drills. This eliminates the possibility of slippage.

3.11 Tools For Angles & Measurement

It's been said that you can weigh twice & cut once. The greatest guidance you can get comes from an elderly woodworker. Another piece of advice is to invest in high-quality, precise, and easy-to-read measurement devices. As a beginner woodworker, you'll require the following measurement and angle-checking tools:

Squares

Without a variety of squares, it's almost difficult to make good woodworking projects. You can construct and check all kinds of angles with good squares. Measuring marks are etched on the top of most squares. As a result, they may even be used as measuring guidelines. You should have the following squares:

- Framing Squares are large, right-angle tools that can be used on larger work surfaces.
- Smaller, right-angle hand instruments called Try Squares are used to easily check squareness.
- Combination Squares are used to verify angles and distances precisely.
- Speed Squares allows you to quickly scan 90-degree and 45-degree angles.
- Miter Squares are the best tools for making angled miter cuts.
- Bevel Squares reconstruct an internal angle & movement patterns using these tools.
- While dividers, compasses, and depth gauges aren't actually squares, they're useful woodworking tools nevertheless. They're related to the other kind of measurement tapes & rules.

Measurements with Tape

At least a tape measure should be attached to the belt of a woodworker.

Since there are so many different kinds of tape measures, it will be difficult to get any of them stuck to you. The following are several simple tape steps to think about:

- The most famous measurement instruments are retractable steel tapes. They are available in lengths ranging from 12 to 30 feet.
- Fabric or steel flexible reel tapes in lengths of over 100 feet are available.
- Folding Rules are not named kings for a reason. There are rigid measurement sticks with a high degree of precision. The majority of rules are divided into several parts.
- Yardsticks & straight edges are rulers that are useful for fast takeoffs & laying straight lines.

Chapter 4: The Best Types of Wood

Have you ever seen a woodworking project on the internet that you wanted to try? You have to know which kind of wood suits well for the project you're working on, whether it's a decorative art piece or a piece of furniture. Different types of wood have varying colors & properties, making them suitable for a variety of applications.

This chapter would focus on natural woods, although that does not rule out the usage of manufactured woods in woodworking. Because of their versatility and flexibility, many furniture makers & artists use hardboard & MDF for specific designs. However, it's crucial to know about the more famous natural species used in woodworking.

4.1 Pine

Pine is a softwood type that is very simple to deal with. Carving and drilling are also simple tasks with pine. Pine has a light yellow color that can brighten up any room. Pinewood is really simple to dye once it has been sealed if you like it to look even darker. Many woodworkers, on the other hand, literally seal the wood & apply a clear finish.

4.2 Cedar

Another softwood that is simple to work with is cedar. It's renowned for its lovely herbal note and soft red tones. It's also very weather resilient. As a result, it's an excellent pick for the furniture that can be placed outdoor. It is also great for storage of clothes that don't get used as much in chests/wardrobes. One should know that moths are normally repelled by wood.

4.3 Redwood

Redwood is also weather tolerant, making it an excellent option for outdoor furniture. It's a soft material that's easy to deal with. It has a reddish tinge to it. Redwood may be stained and painted, but because of its lovely color, many woodworkers opt for a water repellant of mildewcide for outdoor furniture.

4.4 Cherry

Cherry is a much more complex hardwood to deal with. It is, though, regarded as a softer hardwood. It has a reddish hue that goes along with lighter interiors.

4.5 Maple

There are two types of maple trees: one that is harder and one that is softer. If you're new to the game, we suggest starting with the softer kind. The harder wood is extremely difficult to deal with and can only be handled by skilled individuals. Maple is a very resilient wood, making it an ideal choice for any furniture item.

Chapter 5: Maintenance of the Tools

Woodshop tool maintenance, in the most basic form, literally means having the tools functioning as do they did when you first got them out of the package. That's a must-have for any shop that wants to be safe and successful. A decent tool maintenance routine, on the other hand, will lead you much farther. Taking a few extra precautions to care about your tools' cutting edges, work surfaces, alignment mechanisms, & moving parts will make a huge difference in their efficiency. You will increase the efficiency of your woodworking equipment beyond like-new status by adding a few inexpensive power tool upgrades. We will demonstrate to you how to move beyond the basics to keep your shop's tools sharp, genuine, clean, and running smoothly in the subsections below.

5.1 Keeping the Blades Sharp

The majority of instruments in a woodshop are made to do one thing: cut wood. Holding cutting edges as smooth as possible is, of course, one of the most critical facets of tool maintenance. In reality, doing great work here is critical to the safety & the quality of the woodworking. There's a lot you can do to earn yourself the "edge" whenever it comes to cutting & machining pieces, from using hand tool sharpening systems to actually outfitting the equipment with the best saw blades & router bits.

5.2 Circular Saw Blades

Most experienced woodworkers buy parts and blades from suppliers they know and trust. Freud and Forrest's circular saw blades are made of the finest quality carbide & tool steel and are built to maintain their edge over time. These companies often make blades that can withstand applications that are hard on cutting edges, such as cutting man-made substrates & laminates. It's really the only way to get a fresh edge on a saw blade (circular) without costing a specialist sharpening service - it's really easier in the long term to invest a bit more on blades that will go a long while between sharpening.

5.3 Router Bits

When router bits get quite dull or fried, they normally need to be replaced. That's a compelling excuse to avoid bargain parts and bit packs. Rockler's router parts, as well as those from reliable manufactures including Amana & Freud, are made from the finest quality carbide & tool steel, allowing them to last for years without having to be replaced.

5.4 Band Saw Blades

A band saw blades; another cutting instrument that is almost never sharpened is almost often replaced. Replace the band saw blade with the luxury blade on a regular basis as part of your routine maintenance. In the long term, you'll save money and time.

5.5 Drill bits

What about drill bits, for example? Again, the only remedy for a dull drill bit dilemma is to start with the best range of bits one can afford. If used properly, a decent range of Forstner pieces can last a long time before losing their edge. However, even the finest drill bits wear out after a certain period of usage, & a dull drill bit will result in ragged hole-edges & burning. If you're the one that prefers to rush through drilling procedures leaving nothing except crisp, spotless holes in the wake, a sharpening machine like the drill Doctor, which deals for most famous drill bit types, will be a wise tool maintenance investment.

5.6 Hand Tools

Planes, chisels, gouges, & other hand tools necessitate the use of a proper sharpening system. You will grind the tool to the desired shape & refine this to a near-perfect edge with a proper sharpening system for the fragile cutting edges of the finest hand tools. A grinder with cool-running aluminum oxide (white) grinding wheel & a relatively easy honing device, such as Rockler's Plate Glass Sharpening System, will produce perfectly satisfactory results.

Consider spending in a more sophisticated sharpening method if you use a lot of hand tools in your woodworking. At an inexpensive price, the Delta Sharpening Station is also an outstanding all-in-one sharpening machine. It doesn't get much easier than that of the Tormek Sharpening System if you want the best of the best.

5.7 Keeping the Tools Align

Maintaining correct synchronization of woodworking instruments and equipment is critical to their efficiency and accuracy. Quality woodworking equipment once mounted up and tuned, usually remains in sync for a long time. Even the strongest equipment, though, can inevitably get out of adjustment due to friction and continued use. A book or DVD devoted to a certain power tool may be very useful in this situation. All of them have specific instructions about using the tool as well as how to stay in top shape. Although we can't go through every woodworking machine's modification and alignment in-depth, we can make some recommendations for two of the most commonly used equipment in the store.

5.8 Table Saw Alignment

It also benefits to provide a product to help hold items lined up for the focal point of your store, "the table saw." The blade of a table saw must be positioned to operate parallel with the miter slot & fence in order to make straight cuts to prevent safety hazards. The Super Bar table saw of the Master Plate calibration device will assist you in diagnosing alignment issues and ensuring that the table saw blade runs true.

One of the simplest approaches to increase the efficiency of your table saw is to upgrade the fence & miter gauge. Many contractor-grade saws have outstanding specific parts - the bed & motor are perfect - but a high-quality fence & miter gauge aren't often included with the bundle. Many table saws' performance and durability can be significantly improved by introducing an accurate fence system & a precision miter gauge.

5.9 Band Saw Alignment & Tracking

An update to your band saw's blade guiding system will boost its capacity to create a true cut without wander. Many band saws' tracking accuracy can be greatly improved by simply installing a series of ceramic guide blocks. With the addition of a Carter Band Saw Guide, an ordinary band saw may be transformed into a professional-grade machine.

5.10 Keeping Tools Clean & Smooth

Since friction is the adversary in woodworking, keeping the tools clean and clear of pitch & resin accumulation is critical. Although an effective dust removal device would still be the first line of protection against woodworking debris, you'll always require to keep power tool interfaces that come into touch with the wood clean and well lubricated.

How to Keep Saw Blades Clean

It does not take long for the table saw blade to become coated in pitch & resin, particularly when cutting pitchy softwoods. Drag, vibration, & an accumulation of excess heat are both caused by the sticky residue, which affects not just the woodworking expertise, but also the consistency of the cut. The circular saw blades will stay clean and smooth with a couple of squirts of Pitch & Resin Remover & a quick polish at the time of blade change.

Router Bits: Cleaning and Conditioning

The router bits are just another item that should be cleaned on a regular basis. Resin accumulation will greatly increase the friction produced during the cut since there is always just a limited amount of separation b/w a router bit's edge of cutting and its body. To make your router parts bright & shiny, use the same cleaner you use for the saw blades. Grab the router bit & saw blade cleaning kit for long-term safety. A plentiful supply of pitch & resin remover, as well as a lubricant specifically formulated to condition & protect router bit pilot bearings, are included in the kit.

Surfaces with Stationary Tooling

The workpiece is supported by the surfaces of the jointer, table saw, band saw, & planer, which enables it to slip easily through the cut. These surfaces must be maintained clean and corrosion-free in order to work at their best. Most woodworking experts recommend lubricating them lightly to improve their efficiency. The Boesheild tool care kit (3-part) comes with all you'll need to return your tools' work surfaces to their original stain & corrosion-free state, remove pitch & resin, & lubricate them with the lubricant made specifically for power tool care.

Maintaining the Tools Smooth Operation

You have a fantastic chance to develop your woodworking skills and still assisting your equipment in aging gracefully. Power tools, at least decent ones, are designed to withstand intense usage, but you must maintain their mechanical parts if you expect them to last a lifetime. Try to ensure that all of the tools & machinery are in good working condition and are properly lubricated to protect your investment. Aside from the fundamentals, there are several mechanical upgrades that, in certain instances, can increase a power tool's efficiency above that of new.

Bearings & Moving Parts Lubrication

The lubricant one uses to hold the moving parts and bearings of your equipment in good working order should be specifically made for the job. The bearing lubricant penetrates bearings, protecting and sealing internal components, reducing heat buildup, and extending tool lifespan. Lubricate all bearings & moving parts on a daily basis to ensure long, trouble-free operation from all of the stationary and portable power tools. A blade lubricant stick will also help the band saw, scroll saw, & coping saw blades work better. The lubricant stick, made of a specific mixture of wax & oils, improves blade life & helps avoid clogging.

Keeping Up With Tool Maintenance

It's much better to build and commit to a tool repair schedule in the long run than it is to retrieve and restore resources that have been ignored. Make a maintenance schedule for yourself and adhere to it.

Chapter 6: Woodworking Projects for Beginners

There are few projects to get you started on your woodworking path. They are simple to obey and inexpensive, keeping in mind the needs of newcomers to this area. So, without further ado, let's get started.

6.1 Wooden Chopping Board & Serving Tray

Constructing a wood cutting board can be a great weekend project.

Looking for a nourishing woodworking project? Create this beautiful walnut and maple serving tray /cutting board. It is so simple that one can begin in the morning, and then complete it by the afternoon.

Time: 24 Hr. **Skill:** Beginner **Cost:** Approximately $20

Steps for making a wood cutting board

Study how to make the cutting board of your own with the subsequent step-by-step guidelines.

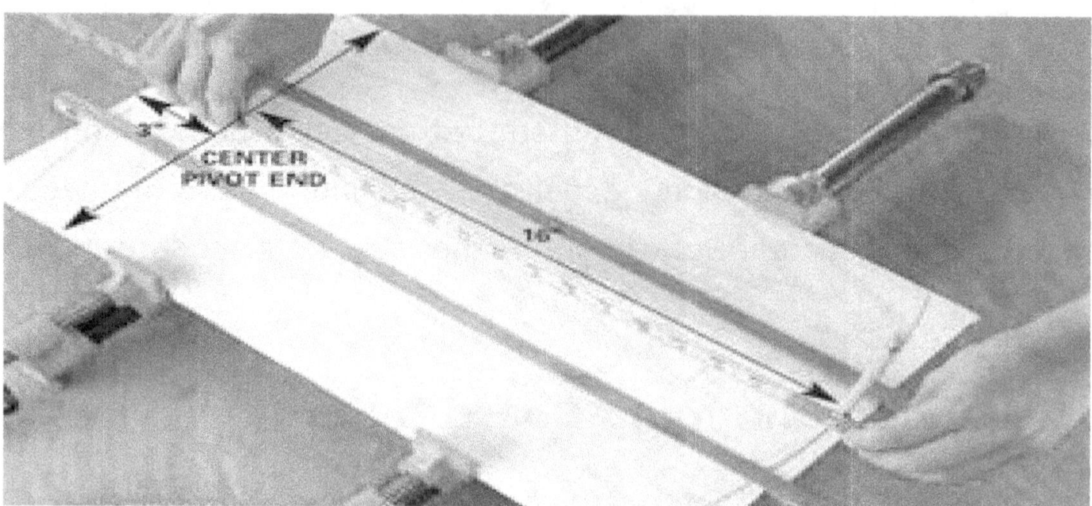

Photo 1: Mark the curves

Drill 1/2-inch holes 3/4 inch from the tips of the walnut strips, centered. Then, with all five boards lightly clamped together, scribe the arcs upon on ends.

Photo 2: Assemble

Remove the boards from the clamp and saw & sand the arcs across each board before gluing the assembly together, keeping the dowel handles unglued.

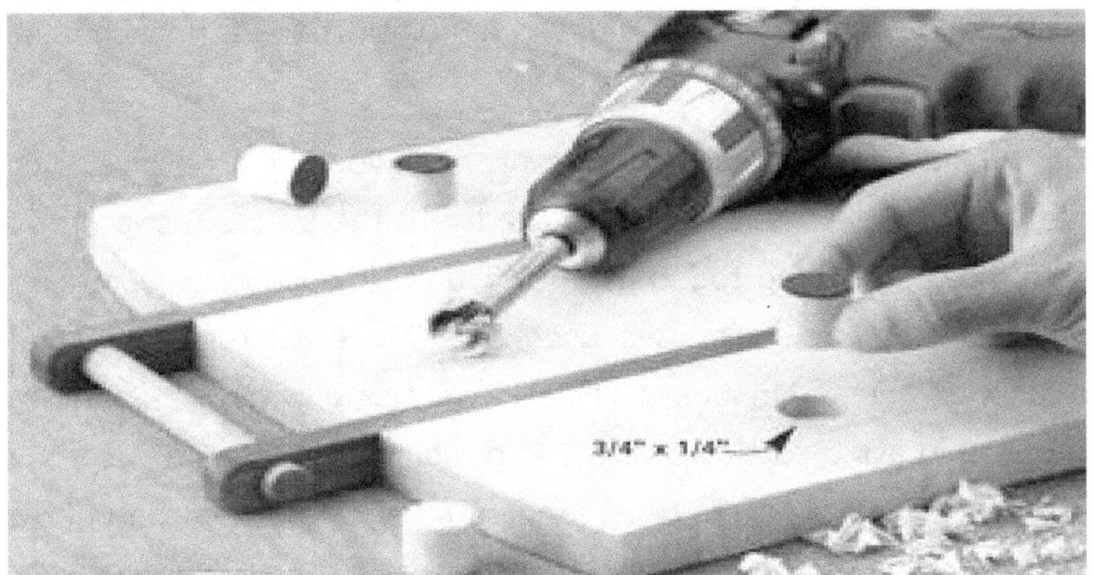

Photo 3: Finish up

Unclamp, sand all sides, and drill a 1/4-inch-deep, 3/4-inch-diameter hole in each corner on the underside. Apply a pair of coats of Oil (Butcher Block) after gluing in the feet & dowel handles. That's it now chop some vegetables.

Chris Ryland's simple, cutting-edge project allows you to slice, dice, & serve in style. We'll teach you how to dry-fit the pieces, scribe the arc, & glue the entire thing together until you start building a wood cutting board. To scribe the arcs, we used a 4-foot steel ruler, however, a yardstick or some thin board will suffice. Using water-resistant wood adhesive and avoid putting the tray in the dishwasher, otherwise, it may break apart. Even, to save time sanding afterward, keep the boards as level as possible during glue-up.

Required Tools for this Project

Have the essential tools for the current DIY project aligned before you begin for saving time & frustration.

- Forstner drill bits
- Cordless drill
- Miter saw
- Jigsaw
- Safety glasses
- Orbital sander
- Tape measure

Required Materials for this Project

Avoid last-minute trips of shopping by having all the materials prepared before time. Take a look at a list.

- Three 20" x 3-1/2" maple boards
- Four ¾" x ¾" diameter dowels (for feet)
- Two 5" x ½" diameter dowels (handles)
- Two 23-1/2" x ½" x ¾" handle strips (walnut strips)

6.2 Build a Shoe Organizer

Organize the shoes in a neat way.

Clean and natural wood racks are ideal for storing shoes off the floor. With no scuff marks or mud buildup on the wall, this basic storage rack can accommodate anything from winter boots to summer sandals.

Time: 60 Mins **Skill:** Beginner **Cost:** Approximately $20

Shoe Rack Plans: Before assembling, cut the pieces

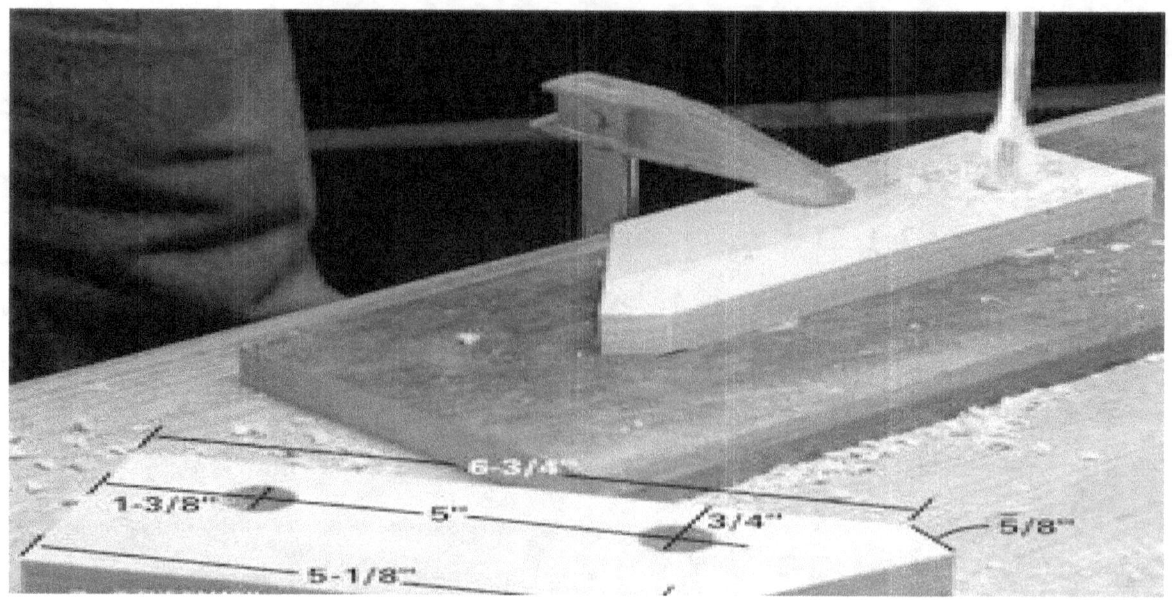

Photo 1: Drilling of dowel holes

Clamp the 1×3 inch support to a portion of wood (scrap) as one drill the holes to avoid the wood from breakage.

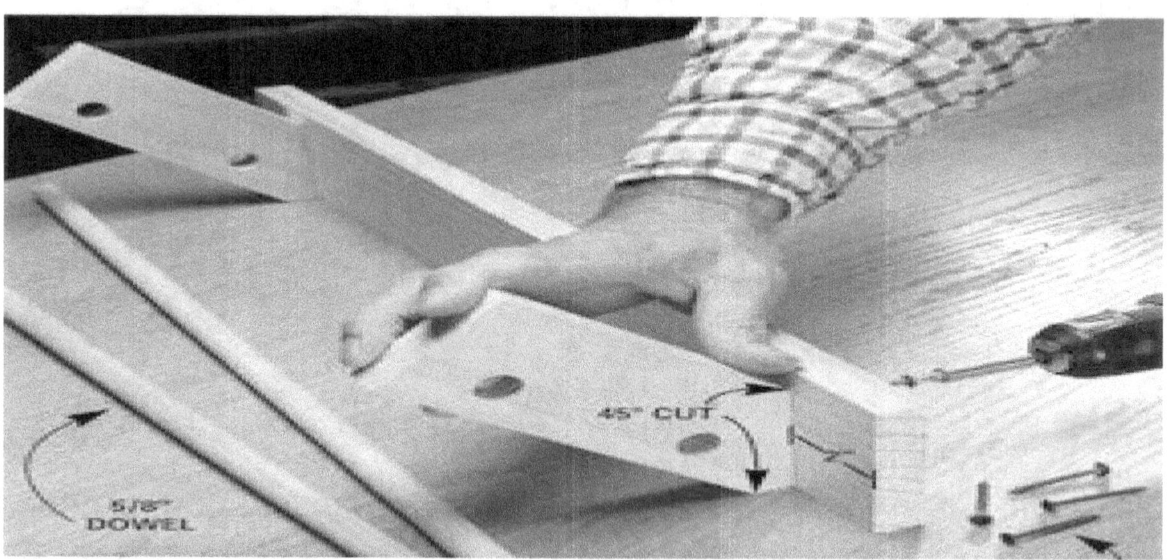

Photo 2: Screwing the pieces together

Drill a hole through the back of 1 x 4 inches into 1 x 3 inches supports before gluing and screwing the bits together.

Shoes appear to pile up in a heap next to entrance doors if extreme caution is not maintained. Remove the tangle with a plain, attractive shoe ladder that holds anything from boots to slippers off the floor and is organized.

The dowel supports are cut and drilled (Photo 1) and screwed to 1x4s (Photo 2). Cut the 1x4s to suit the shoes and the room available—a typical pair of grown-up shoes is 10 inches high. To hang sandals or slippers, glue or nail the dowels through the supports (dowel), leaving 2 in. (or even more) extended afar the supports at the top.

Before you bolt the shoe ladder to a wall, give it a final finish. To keep the shoe ladder in position, screw it to the studs or utilize heavy-duty toggle-bolt type anchors.

Tools Required

Have the essential tools for the current DIY project aligned before you begin for saving time & frustration.

- Clamps
- Screwdriver4-in-1
- Cordless drill
- Level
- Countersink drill bit
- Tape measure
- Miter saw

Materials Required

Avoid last-minute trips of shopping by having all the materials prepared before time. Take a look at a list.

- 1-5/8" screws
- 1x4
- 1x3
- 3" screws for attaching to the wall, or toggle bolts
- Wood glue
- 5/8-in. dowels

Chapter 7: General Safety Rules

7.1 Machine Safety - Ten Commandments

1. Pay attention: The number one source of accidents is not paying attention. Think, think, and think. Maintain your focus on your job. Give your full attention to your job. Do not look about, speak to someone, or utilize a machine after first consciously rehearsing the cut.

2. Keeping machine guards in place at all times: Guards are stationed around you to keep you secure. If a guard was already taken off, inform the instructor so that he or she can replace it before you begin.

3. Don't overreach: Never reach over or across a moving blade.

4. Know your fly zone: Recognize where the wood will go, fly or kick back, if the control is lost, just don't stand in that region. Consider the following scenario: The wood can rotate clockwise in a drill press, so on the left should be the long side. Standing on the right of a table saw can cause the wood to be thrown backward.

5. Properly use the tool: Just use a tool for the purpose for which it was designed. Grain direction, cross-cuts, rip-cuts, blade direction, & proper blade installation are all things to be aware of. When you're done with a tool, switch it off & wait until it comes to a full halt before leaving. Blades are often sensed more than heard.

6. Proper size of the wood: Often incidents occur when anyone tries to cut a portion of the wood that is either too small or too large. The blade rapidly grabs smaller bits of lumber, & the hand carrying the wood immediately leads. The extra force used to force lumber which is too large into the blade will trigger sliding, thrusting, or abrupt escape. After that, body pieces lunge straight onto the hammer. The blade, not the hands, has control over oversized lumber.

7. Approval for special set-up: A particular cut necessitates the removal of guards, which if performed incorrectly, will result in significant injury. Often notify the instructor if you plan on trying a unique set-up.

8. Proper placement of hands: Always have a tight grip on the wood. Always have your arms crossed. Do not slam wood into the blade. Do not yank on the wood. It's possible that you'll trip and fall onto the blade.

9. Keeping the fingers clear: Ensure a space of 2 to 4 inches between the fingers and blades, pinch points, rotating parts, and electrical plugs. Just cut wood that is at least 12" long & 3" wide (the 12/3 rule) to ensure your protection & the safety of others. Prior to cutting any piece shorter than the 12/3 norm, you must notify the instructor.

10. Keep working on the table and against the fence: Until cutting, make sure the wood is squarely between the fencing and the table. Blades & cutters are used to throw, drive, and press wood against both the fence & table. To put it another way, if you don't have wood, the blade can bring it to you, alongside the hand.

7.2 Tid-bit for Safety

Tools that are sharp are safer than dull tools: Make use of sharp materials. Excessive pressure is needed to force dull tools, raising the chance of sliding through a blade. It's often difficult to control dull tools. Sharp tools do just as they're supposed to.

Conclusion

If you want to read more about how to work with wood, you can do a Google search on any of the topics listed, but it is suggested to start with a few helpful books such as this one. In this book, the first two chapters are primarily regarding strategies, while the third focuses on how to pick which hand tools to buy.

Woodworking necessitates the use of all of the senses: sight, scent, listening, sensation, and also tasting (believe us as one can even taste the burning wood). Engage your senses to improve the craft. Engage the senses to ensure your wellbeing.

We want you to enjoy woodworking and be good at doing it. Nothing beats the satisfaction of finishing a project that you produced yourself. Whatever project you're working on, you'll want to make sure you have the correct tools. Many woodworkers desire to engrave or initial piece. We suggest using a Dremel for some painting or engraving if you choose to do this. Whenever you're doing woodworking, make absolutely sure you're remaining safe & having fun.

The woodshop is arguably the most underappreciated industrial arts class. Learning to deal with wood is very valuable for repairing and making items around the home, it also aids you to intermingle with a long convention of craftsmanship. Woodworking was among the first skills created by mankind; the pre-industrial landscape was mostly composed of the tool, & for centuries, all men had a basic knowledge of how to mold and manipulate it. Tradesmen and experts alike had the courage to build cabinets, wooden shelves, and even chairs for their families up till the second half of the twentieth century.

We guarantee that if you devote a little time and effort to studying how to better finish your job, your appreciation of the final product would skyrocket. These finishing touches will entice you to take on yet another project.

Woodworking Projects

The Essential Guide To Learn Woodworking Skills And Use Tools To Create Amazing Projects

By

Jake Wood

Introduction

Woodworking is the process of making or constructing items out of wood. Woodworkers may make items as small as wooden toys or as large as gazebos as a hobby. Woodworking as a hobby has monetary, health, academic, and social advantages.

Woodworking is a financially rewarding hobby. There is a lot of unemployment worldwide, and people who enjoy hobbies like woodworking, gardening, and sawing can use their skills to start businesses related to their hobbies. Employers are also looking for candidates who are enthusiastic about their jobs and have the requisite qualifications. It has been observed that, in the face of significant lifestyle changes and the expression of identities through furniture, art, and handicrafts, carpenters are in high demand, and those who engage in this craft as a hobby or as a profession open themselves up to a wide range of career opportunities and financial success. Woodworking as a hobby, interestingly, provides people with "do-it-yourself" skills, allowing them to complete various woodworking tasks on their own, saving money and time.

Woodworking improves planning skills and raises awareness of health and safety issues. A woodworker must prepare materials, equipment, time, and design, among other things, in order to finish a given task properly. As a result, woodworkers are in a strong place to develop their organizational and preparation skills. Since woodworking necessitates the use of sharp tools and dangerous equipment, woodworkers are taught to be aware of and concerned about the safety of both individuals and machinery. Woodworkers who are passionate about their jobs often invest time learning about safety and health problems, which they can extend to various other fields and professions. Woodworking is a practical ability that can be ideal for people who have difficulty with conventional academic subjects and professions. Training and practicing the skills used in woodworking will help even those who aren't very good at it become master woodworkers, regardless of academic ability. Furthermore, since woodworking requires many measurements and designs, it may aid in the development of mathematical skills. As a result, this craft is both a brilliant profession and a delightful hobby.

Chapter 1: What Is Woodworking?

"Woodworking is a skill that entails cutting, shaping, and joining wood to make decorative or functional items."

Woodworking is not a physically challenging activity, and you can work at your own speed. The fundamental principles are easy to grasp, but it's a hobby that will always be new and demanding as your abilities advance. If you enjoy solving problems, you will enjoy woodworking. Each project presents new challenges. It's just a part of the procedure. Producing really cool things for your home with your hands and brain is also satisfying. Woodworking, generally speaking, is a very solitary experience. If you are somewhat of an introvert and enjoy taking on projects from beginning to end, you can enjoy woodworking. Learning to use wood is not just helpful for making and repairing items of the house, but it also helps you interact with a long tradition of craftsmanship. Woodworking was among the first skills created by humanity; the old world was mostly constituted of wood. For a long time, all men had a basic understanding of how to manipulate and shape wood. Professionals and tradesmen alike had the ability to construct wooden shelves, cabinets, and even chairs for their families, until the second half of the twentieth century.

Chapter 2: Evolution Of Woodworking

Every culture in the world has used woodworking art to make useful, beautiful, and elegant artifacts from ancient times.

Greeks, Ancient Egyptians, Chinese and Roman woodwork are all well documented. Woodworking was also prevalent in several other ancient civilizations around the world, using a variety of styles and techniques. Throughout history, primitive weapons for protection and hunting, as well as basic tools for shelter construction, have been used. At the Kalambo Falls on the Kalambo River, archaeological excavations found digging sticks and a wooden club on the Zambian-Tanzanian border.

Over the years, man became better at killing animals for food, clearing land using his axe, growing crops, and constructing vessels, houses, and furniture as his woodworking skills improved. As a result, woodworking became an essential skill in the development of civilizations.

In the 1800s, woodworking became very common. In the 1880s, secondary schools began offering "industrial arts" classes, and thus, for the following century, taking up a course in mechanics, printing, drafting, or woodworking was a popular educational journey for young men.

Then, starting several decades earlier, shop classes were phased out of secondary school curricula. Schools started to eliminate electives, introduce tougher graduation standards, and concentrate more on college preparation academics and the subjects required for passing state exams as educational resources decreased and the emphasis on standardized tests increased. Since there was no money or time to maintain equipment and workshops, school districts began to eliminate shop classes, assuming that students interested in trade skills could pursue them later at a technical college. This is a shame, since shop classes were never exclusively for the purpose of training students for trade jobs. Rather, whether a carpenter or a doctor, all men were taught manual skills that could be taken advantage of and appreciated throughout their lives. They were seen as essential to developing a well-rounded man who could utilize both his mind and hands.

Woodworking has evolved from a simple necessary skill to something almost mystical or awe-inspiring in our age of factories. Since most 21st-century customers are accustomed to driving to big stores to buy another mass-produced furniture replacement whenever their chair or desk breaks, any man who can walk up to a heap of lumber with a saw and plane to form a beautiful and long-lasting replacement is regarded as a "real craftsman."

Chapter 3: Woodworking tools

The broad range of equipment commercially available can be overwhelming for new woodworkers. It's quick to stock your shop with thousands of dollars worth of costly woodworking equipment. Most beginner woodworker tools, on the other hand, do not have to be extensive or expensive. Following is a list of tools that someone must have in their workshop if they intend to complete their projects properly.

- Sanders
- Chisels
- Files
- Hammer
- Clamps
- Square
- Sawhorses
- Workbench
- Mallet
- Drill
- Screw Gun
- Tape Measure
- Power saws
- Hand saws
- Planes

Basic woodworking tools are classified into five basic types according to the functions they perform. These are instruments for:

- Cutting
- Finishing
- Assembling

- Measuring

- Holding wooden pieces

as they are transformed from raw materials to finished products. These tool groups include all a beginner woodworker would need to construct simple to complex objects.

In the following paragraphs, we will explain some of the most basic tools and their uses in woodworking.

1.   The Hammer

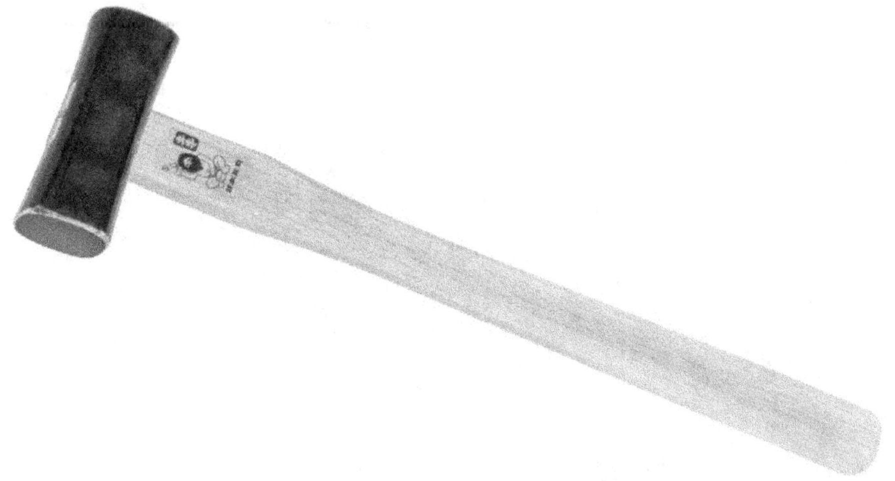

A slab of metal on top of a stick screams blunt force. It's possible that this is the oldest method in the book. We recall seeing a photo of a man with his hammer arsenal when we first began woodworking; it was a whole large room with numerous different hammers. We didn't think I'd ever need more than one at the time, but things have changed since then. As we write this, nine hammers are visible in my mind. - one is special, and they're all used on a regular basis. My personal favorite is the one seen above. It's a Japanese carpenter's hammer weighing 375 gr. The flat side is for driving nails, while the convex side pushes the nail underneath the surface. From pushing chisels and modifying planes to clicking joints and shutting containers, we utilize it for everything. It's the hammer we still reach for. The weight is just right, and we like the way it hangs. A claw hammer could be a safer option if your job requires a lot of nailing. I'd stick with this choice and add an additional pry bar to my set. When doing lighter slicing with a claw hammer, try driving the chisel with the sides of the hammerhead rather than the face. You'll have more power and a greater striking area as a result.

2.   Chisels

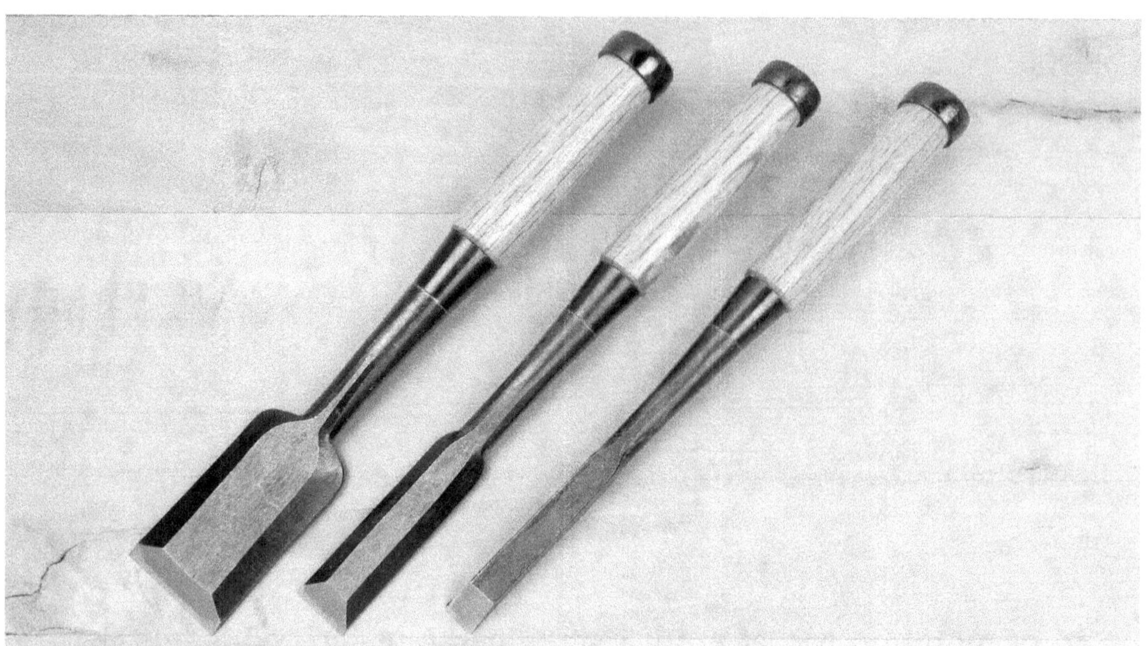

The chisel is next in line. It's capable enough to do anything from heavy chopping to light trimming and fine carving. While it can be used to turn screws, open paint cans, and serve like a pry bar, but those aren't recommended applications. Use a screwdriver, please. Although there are dozens of different sizes and types of chisels, most people only need four. Standard bench chisels in 1/4, 1/2, 3/4, and 1 inch are recommended. Choose ones that are comfortable to hold and learn, sharpening them. There are almost no chisels that are ready to be used right out of the box; they all require some sharpening to perform at their best. Once you've used a genuinely sharp chisel, you'll appreciate the difference, not just in terms of what you can do but also in terms of how simple it is to do so. A heavily patterned chisel known as atsu-nomwe(thick chisel) is shown above, which is used for splitting joints in big timbers. It's one of my favorites from a collection made for me by professional blacksmith Lyoroi.

3.   Hand Planes

Hand planes were traditionally used for smoothing and changing the width of the rough board (a process known as "thickness"). While some people tend to work this way, machines do the majority of the heavy lifting when it gets to dimensioning stock. This isn't to say that now the hand plane is no longer useful. It's always a fantastic tool that no craftsman should be without. A very well-hand plane can do in mins what a sander can do in an hour while still producing an arguably better surface. It also encourages you to work instead of working in a cloud of dust or sitting in a pile of shavings. If we had to pick only one, I'd go with a low-angle block plane such as this one. It can be used for anything from shaving and designing stock to finishing planning surfaces, and it's pretty simple to install and sharpen. They're seldom ready to use right out of the box, just like chisels. They can be seen as a package that must be completed before they can be used.

4.   Hand Saw

Most of the work that a saw does has been taken over by the electric version, just as it has been taken over by the hand plane. Nonetheless, the handsaw is still an important tool for every woodworker's toolkit. Crosscut and rip saws are the two most common types of wood-cutting saws. Rip saws have fewer, larger teeth and are designed to cut in the direction of the grain. Crosscut saws are used to cut through the wood, as the name suggests. To prune the grain and leave a cleaner cut, they usually have more and finer teeth. Although combination and general-purpose saws are available, they are often too violent for delicate work. A Japanese ryoba nokogirweis a preferable hand saw. It has crosscut teeth on the one hand and rip-teeth on the other, and it cuts on the pull stroke, unlike western saws. These used to be hard to come by, but now you can usually find them in home improvement shops.

5.   Clamps

Almost any process with the tools described becomes more complicated without clamps. They're useful not only for holding the final assembly together but also for keeping stuff where you want them as you work. Nothing is more aggravating than attempting to deal with a bit of wood that slips around. Clamps are important, and most carpenters have heard the phrase "you can never have too many clamps" at least once in a lifetime. Much of the time, they wish for more. Two 24'' bar clamps will suffice. Four is preferable. Eight is even better...

Chapter 4: Woodworking skills

We accept that perfecting the craft of woodworking is difficult, but believe me when we say that it is also not a mystery. If you've been putting off tackling your dream DIY project due to a lack of faith, now is the time to break free!

Until we get into the details, I'd like to send you a few pointers that you should keep in mind as a beginner. These will assist you in navigating this vast ocean of woodworking with ease.

- Begin with small projects- Begin with outside projects to hone your woodworking skills because the demand for perfection in a wooden dog house isn't as big as it could be in a new sofa table.

- Be inspired- Browsing the photos of completed projects will motivate and inspire you to be more innovative.

- Create a workplace suited to your liking- You must ensure that you have a secure and sufficient workspace for carpentry. Finding a spot in your house where you can create noise and use your equipment can be difficult but is essential.

- Devise a plan and implement- Planning ahead of time allows people to work on their project more efficiently. It saves one from being caught in any holes. You'll have a description of all the equipment you'll need, as well as the number of supplies, budget, and time you'll need ahead of time. This allows you to save more time and remain on track to complete the project on time. Always note your fundamentals and use them when no other techniques are available. Learn from your mistakes, and one job at a time, your abilities will be polished. The trick is to love what you're doing; if you're enthusiastic enough, you'll be a pro in no time.

- Selecting the appropriate equipment- To get started, gather some simple hand tools and a few machine tools. This way, you won't spend all your money and will have the option of purchasing more sophisticated equipment as your business grows.

- Have a good time and be creative- Start experimenting rather than sticking to the blueprint. There will be setbacks, so don't give up. You will eventually create something new, something original, and unique!

- Look for a mentor- Join local woodworking groups to get some assistance or find someone who can guide you.

Let's learn some fundamental skills that will help you feel more secure now that you've mentally prepared to board. These valuable lessons will assist you in realizing that you can complete several carpentry tasks using inexpensive or exotic tools.

1. Cutting Materials

One can cut the wood in various ways, including with a table saw, a jigsaw, circular saws, and other tools. A hand saw and a jigsaw, on the other hand, are the most economical and serve for 85-90 percent of the projects, in my experience.

- Hand Saws- These are ideal for making fast, straight cuts that don't require a great deal of precision. They'll probably make you sweat because they're not driven. While it is ideal for beginners who don't want to spend a lot of money and want to get things done quickly, it has the drawback of requiring different saws for various materials. As a result, you will incur an extra expense, but it will not be excessive.

- Jig Saw- Jigsaw puzzles can be used for almost any project. It's a perfect all-around saw with a reciprocating tip. They're not great for making perfectly straight cuts, but they're great for making irregular cuts and curves. These blades are inexpensive, lightweight, and easily exchangeable when cutting a variety of materials.

- Circular saw- If you want to make more precise cuts, you can use a circular saw, which is very heavy and needs the skills of a professional woodworker. They're ideal for cutting long, straight, and precise lines in a variety of materials.

2. Drilling Holes

Drilling holes is a necessary part of almost any do-it-yourself project. You'll get the best results using a wireless drill, which is highly efficient, long-lasting, and inexpensive. They assist you in various tasks, from drilling holes of every size into various materials to tightening screws. While using a drill is very easy, there are a few techniques and tips that you can learn to help you use it more effectively and get the best out of it.

3. Realize how wood behaves

Before you use any tool on your lumber, you must first determine its proper direction and orientation in which one should plane the board. Ring layers begin to develop around one another as trees mature and grow up, resulting in beautiful grain in our boards. If we neglect the best working course, this grain will make planing more difficult. Working with wood grain is similar to petting a cat: if you go from tail to head, the fur may stand straight up, and you will get hissing disapproval, but if you go from head to tail "with the grain," the hairs will lay aside smoothly, and a purr of approval will be heard.

It's also crucial to know how wood contracts and expands as humidity levels change throughout the year. This natural property is taken into account in all wooden buildings, and ignorance of it can be catastrophic.

4. Sharpen Planes, Saws and Chisels

So many people have propagated the misconception that working with wood by hand is extremely difficult due to the sole reason of using a dull tool. It would be best if you made it a habit of sharpening your blades. Since using rusty tools can be hazardous and ineffective, it is among the essential fundamental skills. There is a common axiom among woodworkers that you must "let the tool do the work" so that things run smoothly. You must realize that if your saw needs a lot of force to cut or requires a running start to shave, you are doing it incorrectly.

5. Choosing the right screws

If you need to attach stuff, screws are the best option. There are hundreds of them in various sizes, so deciding which one to use for your craft projects can be difficult.

As a novice, you should be aware of the most popular styles so you can choose one to use for your current or future project.

- Sheet Metal Screws- Because sheet metal is slim, they are usually shorter than wood screws. Even though they are self-tapping, a pilot hole is still needed. They are connected to the head and have a fine pitch.
- Wood Screws- They have a flat head, coarse pitch, and an unthreaded shank. They have a good grip on the wood and can even rest flat against it. Before screwing it into the wood, most of them need a pilot hole, which you can create with a drill bit.
- Machine Screws- These are available in various sizes and shapes, but they have a higher strength than others since they are

machined. They are made up of fine threads. To mount these screws, you'll need to use a nut/bolt.

- Drywall Screws- Like wood screws, these are generally longer having rough threads.

6.Sanding

Cutting and drilling holes to complete a job is insufficient because it leaves splinters and shrapnel on the surface. The wood can be sanded to repair this. It can be a little confusing with all of the various types of sandpaper and sanding equipment available.

Here are the most popular sanders for sanding wood, along with a brief description of how they work:

- Belt Sanders- These sanders are the most strong and heavy-duty. With the sandpaper belt wrapped around them, they can get through a lot of material easily. They can be used for projects with a wide flat surface.
- Hand Sanders- Hand sanders are the most basic of all, and they're ideal for beginners and small projects. It includes a handle to which the sandpaper is attached at the bottom and a plate. It has the advantage of being the cheapest, but it has the disadvantage of taking a little longer. It will, however, undoubtedly assist you in achieving a flawless finish.
- Orbital Sanders- These are ideal for small and cramped spaces. They use sanding discs to keep a tight grip on the surface they're working on.
- Sanding along the Grain- You should know how to sand with the grain of the wood as a beginner. By sanding along the grain rather

than against it, you can achieve a smooth finish without leaving any marks.

7.Cutting Dovetail Joints

The dovetail joint is by far the most favored and solid way to connect the board corners when making a box. The wedged formed "tails" with a one-sided cut that goes through the "pins" are involved. Molding or paint is used to conceal the unsightly joinery.

Forming dovetail joints is now a litmus test for serious woodworkers in recent years, but don't be afraid to give it a shot.

It's a very straightforward procedure.

- Tails should be cut.
- On the other board, trace the tails.
- The waste you identified should then be cut out.

8.Cutting a Mortise and Tenon Joint

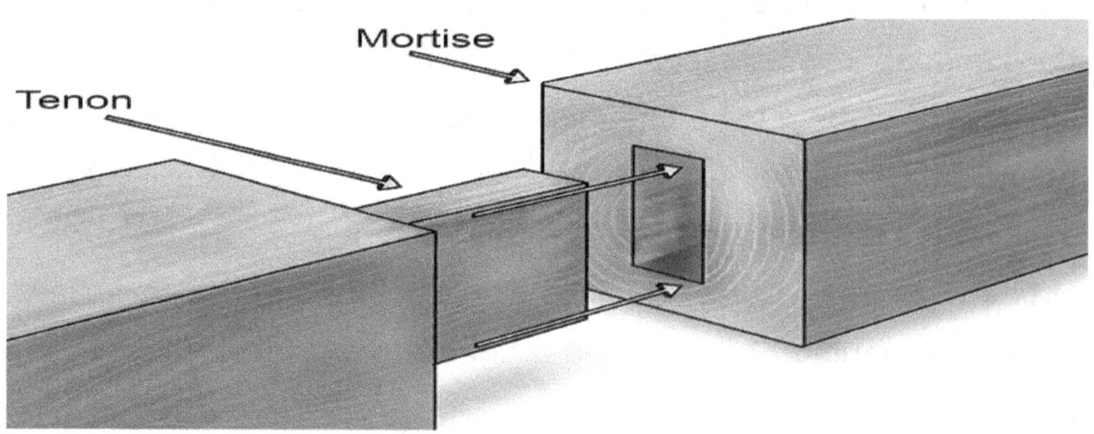

In the world of carpentry, the mortise joint is perhaps the most basic. Interlocking horizontal and vertical bits at 90 degrees may be used to connect them. This is accomplished by inserting a tenon into the mortise. A strong understanding of how to use the technique will help you achieve a comfortable, snug fit. Making a mortise and determining the width of the tenon can be done in a variety of ways. A few simple cuts with a saw are all that is needed to cut the tenon.

If you practice how to build this joint properly, the gates to the realm of woodworking will unlock and welcome you. As a result, make certain you understand it correctly.

9. Painting & Finishing the product

After you've spent hours designing your perfect project, the next step is finishing it and giving it a professional appearance.

Finishing creates a glamorous appearance while still protecting the integrity of the construction. So, my recommendation is not to skimp on this.

For their designs, people use a variety of finishes. Shellac is used by others, while others use paint. A good paint is typically the basic finish. There are 2 kinds of popular paints, and the one you use depends on what type of material you'll be painting on.

- Oil-based Paint- The paint adheres to surfaces easier, but cleanup is more difficult. It's best to use it while you're painting on an oil-based paint coat.
- Latex Paint- It's water-based paint that can be used in a variety of applications. It's easy to clean with only soap and water. It's also long-lasting and simple to apply to various materials.

Once you've decided on a paint color, you'll need to decide on a sheen (gloss to flat). A flat paint finish will mask flaws better, while a shiny finish will last longer.

Chapter 5: Woodworking Projects

To most people, a chair, whether handcrafted or not, is simply a structure that keeps the buttocks from touching the ground, but it is much more to the woodworker. To him, the handcrafted chair is a precious artifact of human genius. A chair made by the skilled hands of a dedicated woodworker becomes much more than that. Its curves, scent, and rich colors combine to create a usable extension of the house that speaks for itself and invites people passing to sit and appreciate one of life's greatest pleasures: relaxation. The art of woodworking encompasses far more than the production of commonplace objects. It is a highly specialized skill that generations of artisans learn and consider to be a form of art in its own right. Woodworking has surpassed the art forms such as drawing, painting and photography as a practice that has a rich connection with age, the physical senses, and usability; three realms that show a hearty comprehension of human values that go beyond the temporal limits of existence, since its inception out of the transition from nomadic civilizations to settled cultures.

Such is the concept and importance of woodworking. In this book, as we move further, we will learn how to make some of the most exotic and perfect artifacts. These may be of use outside one's home or inside.

Chapter 6: Indoor Woodworking Projects

Who doesn't enjoy adding decorative elements to their home? But rather than buying something off the shelf, why not create something from scratch? As a result, we've compiled a list of DIY projects with which you can try to improve the look of your home. A few of the works are so simple that even novices may complete them. They are as follows:

1. Cedarwood Bath Mat

We saw a cedarwood mat similar to this for $35 on the internet and thought to myself, "Hey, we can create a fantastic one for less." You can make one in three simple steps as well.

Time: 1 hour

Difficulty: Beginner

Cost: 23 dollars

Materials Required:

- paint stir stick
- 1x2 or 1x6 lumber
- Sandpaper
- antiskid pads
- finishing supplies
- 1¼ inches nails

Instructions:

- Slats should be cut- If you can't find good-quality 1x2 stock at your local home center, buy a 1x6 and cut 1½-inches strips out of it. All of the slats WEwanted came from an 8-foot 1x6.

- Rounding the corners and edges. With a quarter-inch round-over piece, WErounded the slat edges. If you don't have a router, use 100-grit sandpaper to smooth the edges.

- Set up the Mat. To make a square, clamp wooden scraps to your workbench. Using spacers sliced from a paint stir stick, align the slats against the guide. Then, cut three runners one inch shorter than the mat's width. 1-1/4-inch brads or nails are used to secure the runner to the slats. Besides using paint stir sticks as spacers, see what else you can do with free items from The Home Depot.

Tips:

- We went with cedar because of its aesthetics and rot tolerance. However, any wood would suffice.

- My mat measures 14-1/2 x 30 inches, but you could still make it any size you want. Simply ensure that the slats are covered by runners that are no greater than 15 inches apart.

- Large knots build weak points, so you can need to purchase additional lumber to get knot-free sections.

- Despite the fact that the nail holes would not be visible, we filled these with wood filler prior to sanding and finishing. If the nail heads are left exposed, they can corrode and ruin the floor.

- Tung oil was used to finish my mat. Oil finishes aren't as long-lasting as other types, but they're simple to reapply when they start to wear out—just rub on a fresh coat.

- To prevent the mat from slipping on hard floors, use antiskid padding on the rim.

2. Kitchen Step Stool

If you or somebody you love is vertically challenged, kitchen stools could be extremely useful for accessing upper cabinets. This one has two steps and dowelling for joints, and it's built in the shaker style. The use of a router and model to build the side pieces, however, is an essential step in the construction. Make one for yourself.

Time: A few hours

Difficulty: Intermediate

Cost: 51-100 dollars

Materials Required:

- ¾ inches Baltic Birch Plywood
- 3/8 inches Walnut Dowel
- Wood glue
- ¼-inches plywood

Tools Required:

- Jigsaw

- Router
- Table saw
- dado blade set
- Handsaw
- Clamps

Blueprint:

Figure 1

Figure 2

Stuff to be cut:

Key	Qty	Material	Dimensions	Part
A	2	3/4" Plywood	1/2" x 6" x 10"	Sides
B	1	3/4" Plywood	1/2" x 10"	Top Step
C	1	3/4" Plywood	1/2" x 6" x 10"	Bottom Step
D	12	3/8" Dowel	1/2" x 10"	Dowels
E	1	1/4" Plywood	1/2" x 10"	Side template

Instructions:

- Parts should be milled. Mill the pieces to rough size using the Cutting List as a guide.

- The dadoes and rabbets should be cut. Set your dado up for a 3/4-inch wide, 3/8-inch deep groove. For the bottom stage, cut a ten inches dado from the base of each hand (C).

- Fasten a plywood fence using clamps to your saw's fence so you can slip it right up against the blade to cut the top rabbets. Cut the rabbets at the corner.

- Make a model (E). On a sheet of quarter or half inches plywood, draw the shape of the side (see Fig. 1). Clamp the piece to your workbench and use a jigsaw to cut out the shape. Up to the line, sand the template (E). Take your time and make the template as good as you can. Any flaws in the design would be visible on the completed sides.

- Sides should be rough cut. Trace the outline onto each side's inside face. While tracing its second side of the template to make the left and right bits, make sure to turn it over. Cut each side rough, remaining around 1/4-inch outside the line.

- Rout the sides of the sheet. Use three-quarters inch each eighteen-gauge brad nails to secure the model to one of the sides. To prevent the prototype from raising when routing, retain the nails near to the edge. Trim the edges flush with the model with an upper flush-trim bit with a half-inch shank when clamped to your bench. Perform again on the other side surface, removing the model and brad nails.

- Make a note of the phase angles. Without using glue, clamp the stool together with the bottom stage protruding over both the front and back of the sides. Allow the front edge of the top step to overhang the back of the stool. Shift the angle from the steps' sides to the steps' ends.

- Make the moves slanted. To tear the steps to their final width, tilt your table saw's blade to match the scribed angles on the steps.

- Put the stool together. Fasten the stool together using clamps and search for squareness after gluing the dadoes and rabbets. Using a wet towel, wipe away any leftover glue.

- Drill holes for the dowels. Remove the clamps once the glue has dried and leave a mark to drill the dowel holes. The dowel holes should be uniformly spaced, centered on the thickness of the measures. Using a 3/8-inches bit, drill 2-inches deep holes. To avoid tearing the veneer off the plywood, WEused a Forstner bit.

- Dowels should be mounted. Place a dowel in each hole and glue it in place. The dowels must only be visible above the surface so that you can cut them flush once the glue has dried. Using a handsaw, trim the dowels. Make a hole in a piece of plastic or cardboard and slide it over the dowel to shield the surface from the saw's teeth. Finally, sand the surface.

3.   Foldable Dog Ramp

We all want our dogs to be by our sides, but as they get older and can't jump on to a bed or other places they used to be able to, it can be heartbreaking for their owners. Alternatively, the dog can be too tiny to reach such areas at any point in its lifespan. This dog ramp is a durable, dependable project that takes just an afternoon to complete.

Time: A few hours

Difficulty: Intermediate

Cost: Around 25 dollars

Materials Required:
- 1/4" x 3-1/2" Carriage Bolt (two)
- 2' x 4' 1/2" Plywood
- 8' 1x4 Lumber (four)
- Staples
- 1-1/16" x 12" Continuous Hinge
- 1-1/4" Construction Screws
- 2' x 4' Piece of Carpet
- 2" Construction Screws
- 8' 1x2 Lumber (three)
- 1/4" Nylon Nuts (two)

- 1/4" Washers (four)

Tools Required:

- Miter saw
- Jigsaw
- Staple gun
- Wrench
- Clamps
- Drill/driver

Blueprint:

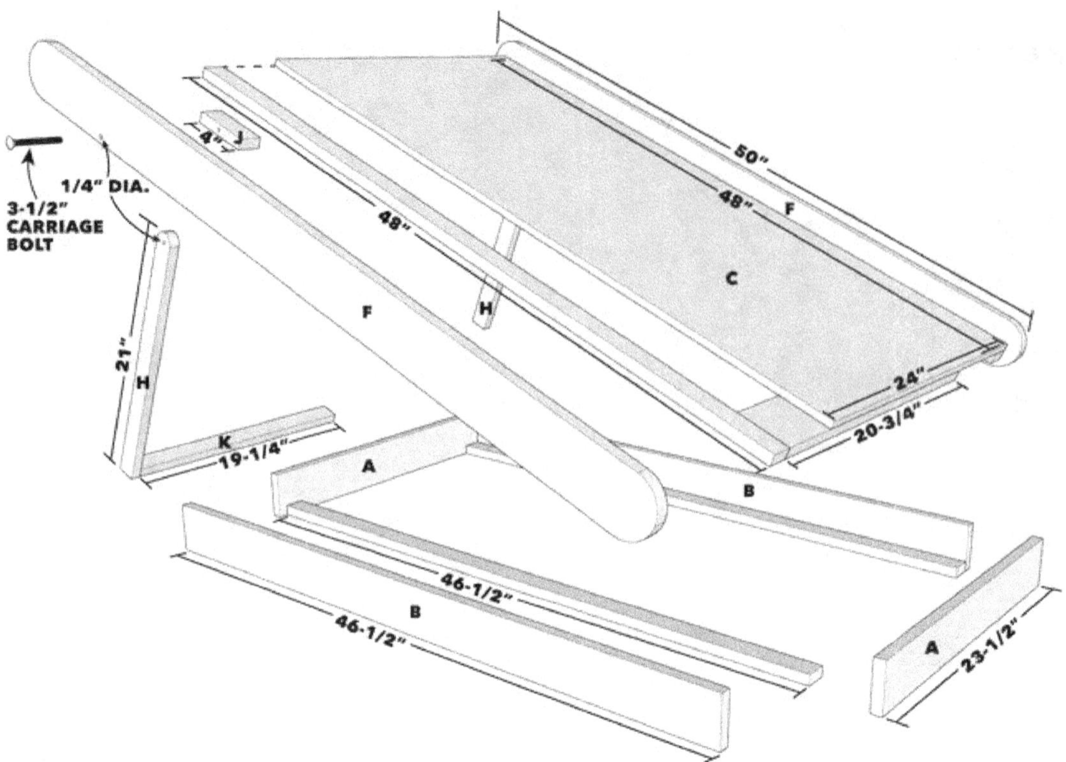

Stuff to be cut:

Key	Qty	Material	Dimensions	Part
A	2	1x4 Board	3/4" x 3-1/2" x 23-1/2"	Short Base
B	2	1x4 Board	3/4" x 3-1/2" x 46-1/2"	Long Base
C	1	1/2" Plywood	1/2" x 24" x 48"	Ramp
D	2	1x2 Board	3/4" x 1-1/2" x 46-1/2"	Ledger
E	1	1x2 Board	3/4" x 1-1/2" x 46-1/2"	Base Runners
F	2	1x4 Board	3/4" x 3-1/2" x 50"	Sides
G	1	1x4 Board	3/4" x 3-1/2" x 20-3/4"	Hinge Support
H	2	1x2 Board	3/4" x 1-1/2" x 21"	Legs
J	2	1x2 Board	3/4" x 1-1/2" x 4"	Leg Support
K	1	1x2 Board	3/4" x 1-1/2" x 19-1/4"	Strut
L	1	Carpet	24" x 48"	Carpet

Instructions:

- Cut the boards down to size. Follow the list and use a miter saw to crosscut your boards to the proper size.

- With a jigsaw, round the ends of the sides (part F). At the ends of the sides, draw 1-3/4-in.-radius circles (part F). To make the arc,

WEtraced a 1-quart measuring cup. Fasten the board using clamps to the work surface and use a jigsaw to cut down the line with low-grit sandpaper, smooth the arcs.

- Assemble the foundation. Drill pilot holes and use 2-in. construction screws to secure the long base parts (B) to the end of the small base parts (A).
- Connect the rest of the foundation to the base supports (part E). These parts will strengthen the foundation and provide a seat for the legs.
- Construct the ramp. Drill pilot holes and use 1¼-inches construction screws to secure the struts (part D) to all the sides of the plywood ramp (part C).
- To get the right spacing, place the ramp on a 3/4-inch scrap piece.
- Fasten the sides (F) against the ramp's edge with pilot holes and 2-inch construction screws. For each face, WEused four screws.
- The hinges are used to secure the ramp to the foundation. Attach the hinge support (part G) to one of the base's short sides. Make a note of the centers and double-check that they line up when clamped.
- Attach the 12-inch hinge to the hinge support as well as the frame.
- Close the hinge and shim the hinge support with a scrap 1x4 and a shim to hold it flat.
- Place the ramp assembly on the foundation, plumb the hinge end, and use five pilot holes and five 1¼-inches construction screws to secure the ramp to the hinge support.
- Legs should be fastened to the ramp. One end of the 1x2 leg pieces should be rounded (part H).
- Drill a 1/4-inch pilot hole at the end of the panels where the two legs meet.

- Attach the leg supports (part J) Three inches from the non-hinge end of the ramp with two 2-in. construction screws.
- Drill a pilot hole in the ramp faces (F) and leg supports with a 1/4-inch bit (J). With 1/4-inches x 3½-inches carriage bolts, 1/4-inches washers, and ¼-inches nylon bolts, clamp the legs Five inches from the end of the ramp to the inner side of the leg supports.
- Stick it to the carpet with a staple. With a knife or cutter, cut the carpet to size (part L). Using a staple cartridge, staple the carpet to the ramp.

4. Chessboard

On this custom-built chessboard, you'll have a blast. It's also quite easy! Choose the complementary wood species you want to use, grab some glue and a few other equipment and supplies, and you're ready to get started.

Time: A few hours

Difficulty: Intermediate

Cost: Around 25 dollars

Materials Required:

- 8' 1x4 Board of Aspen Wood
- 8' 1x4 Board of Mahogany Wood
- 2' x 2' of 1/2" Plywood
- Wood glue
- 1-inches 18-gauge nails

Tools Required:

- Clamps
- Table saw
- 18-Gauge Nail Gun
- Router
- Miter saw

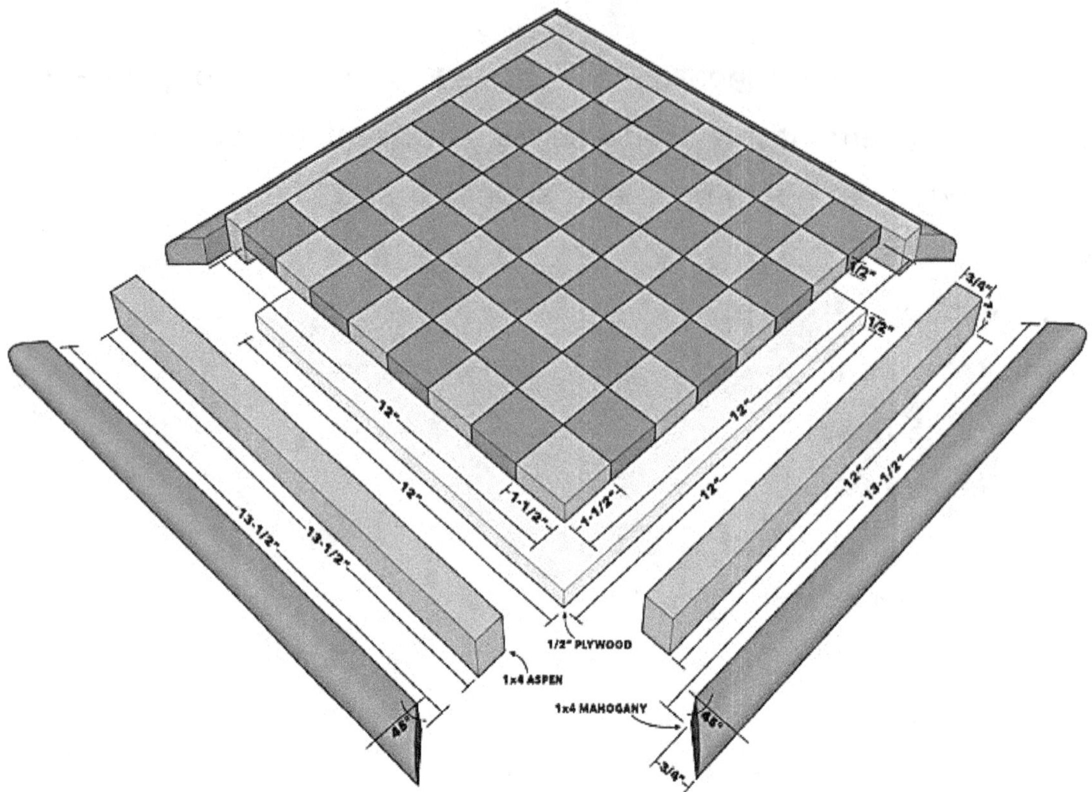

Instructions:

- On the table saw, cut boards to 1-1/2 inches. Although you can buy 1x2 boards and bypass this stage, we don't always expect the edges to be square.

- Using a miter saw, rough-cut the boards. Cut four 16-inch pieces from each ripped wood species. We were using a stop that we wouldn't have to keep measuring over and over. This rough cut can give you some wiggle room when it comes to gluing the pieces together and cutting them into strips.

- Glue the strips together. Alternate dark and light wood while laying out the boards. Ensure the edges are well-aligned. To put it another way, don't rely on clamps to hold the boards together. Apply the wood glue evenly over the surfaces, ensuring that it reaches the edges. Using bar clamps, secure the pieces together. Allow to air dry absolutely.

- Plane or sand the freshly formed board smooth and even with low-grit sandpaper.

- Cut the jagged edges of the board with a miter gauge on the table saw.

- Make a halt and crosscut the board. Set a stop at 1-1/2 inches from the blade and crosscut eight stripes from the surface using the same miter gauge method as before.

- Flip the stripes over and glue them together. Create the chessboard pattern by laying out the stripes and flipping every other strip. Clamp the strips together after gluing them together. Allow to air dry absolutely. The freshly constructed chessboard may be sanded or planed.

- Plywood should be cut and fastened to the chessboard. Calculate the chessboard's dimensions. It's doubtful that it'll be a perfect square, but double-check. Cut your 1/2-inch plywood to the equivalent of your chessboard by ripping and crosscutting it. Clamp the plywood to the game board with glue, clamps, and one-inch 18-gauge nails to produce a smooth bottom surface.

- Rip the wood to the depths. Taking the smallest height from many measurements of the chessboard and rip the lighter type of wood to that size.

- Scribe Wooden Lengths Using the chessboard as a guide, scribe the lengths of the ripped light board. On the miter saw, split the light wood to those lengths. Attach the pieces to the chessboard's edges with glue and brad nails. Sand the chessboard until it is level with the base.

- Dark wood should be rounded over and ripped. To round the edges of the dark wood, use a router and a 1/4-inches round-over bit. On the table saw, cut the board to ¾ inches. If you choose not to do this, home improvement stores sell 3/4-inch quarter-round molding in almost any wood species. These materials are typically inexpensive and can help you save time when it comes to construction.

- Cut a 45-degree angle into the round board with a miter saw. Transfer it to the game board and scribe the length of the outer rim on the other side of the board. To have the other three sides, repeat the process.

- Allow the mitered boards to cure by gluing and clamping them to the chessboard. Make sure to get the glue all the way around the angles. This is crucial for a strong grip. If you don't like the glue, you can secure the chessboard with 1-1/2-inches 18-gauge brad nails.

5. Floating Shelves

Floating shelves can be purchased for $20 to $80 each in stores or online. However, before you do that, think about creating your own. You can get the same size, thickness, and look you want for around the same price. You may also paint them to fit your furniture or trim. Your handmade shelves would also be more durable than most store-bought shelves, as ours can hold up to 50 pounds each. Plus, when you're finished, you'll have a lot of bragging rights.

Time: A few hours

Difficulty: Beginner

Cost: Around 100-250 dollars

Materials Required:

- 4" lag screws
- Stainable wood filler
- Carpenter's glue
- 1" nails (18 gauge)
- 4' x 8' sheet of half-inch plywood (red oak)
- 24" x 96" roll of veneer (for seven or eight shelves)
- Tack cloths
- 1-5/8" (No. 8) wood screws
- Wood stain
- Cotton rags
- Disposable foam paint brushes
- 2×4 board
- Non-hardening wood putty

Tools Required:

- Edge-band trimmer
- Random orbit sander
- Stud finder
- 4-feet level
- Circular saw
- Belt sander
- Nailer
- Drill/driver

Blueprint:

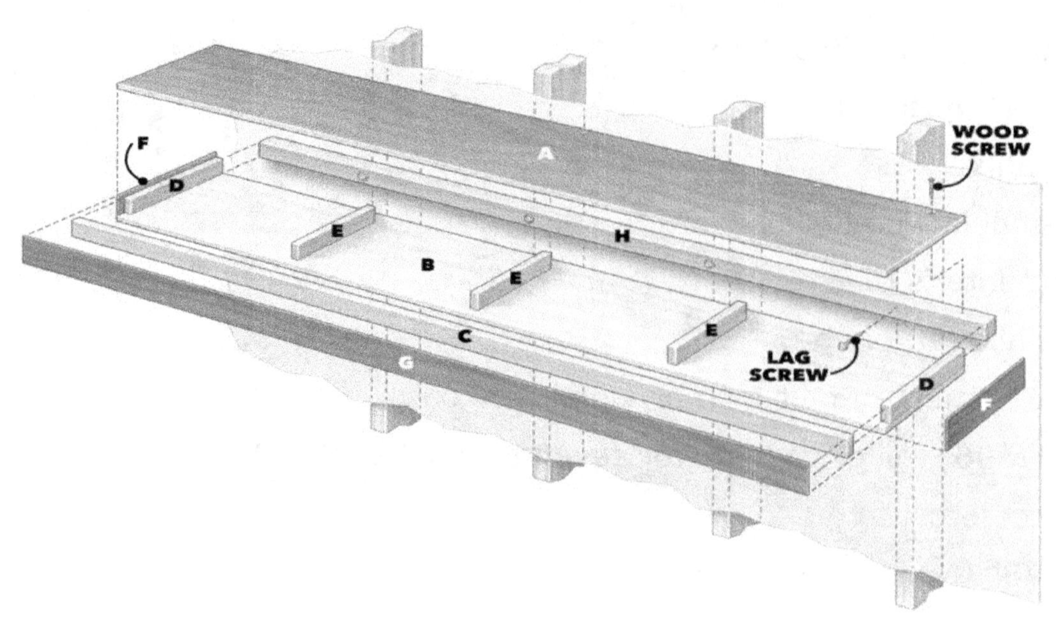

WOOD SCREW
LAG SCREW
A
B
C
D
E
F
G
H

Stuff to be cut:

Key	Qty	Dimensions	Part
A	1	11-1/8" x 72"	Top Panel
B	1	11-1/8" x 72"	Bottom Panel
C	1	1-1/2" x 72"	Front Rail
D	2	10-5/8" x 1-1/2"	Side Rails
E	3	8-1/2" x 1-1/2"	Fillers
F	2	3" x 11-5/8" (Trimmed To Fit)	Side Veneer
G	1	3" x 72-1/2" (Trimmed To Fit)	Front Veneer
H	1	1-3/8" x 1-1/2" x 70-3/4"	Wall Cleat

Instructions:

- A single-plank shelf looks fantastic, but big, thicker planks can be difficult to come by, costly, or both. So, we cheated and used real wood adhesive-backed veneer, which is simple to cut and add and gives the appearance of solid wood.

- We used a self-squaring crosscut guide for short cuts, and for "rip" cuts, we used a longer guide. A small piece of 3/4-inches plywood is mounted on top of a broader piece of 1/4-inches plywood, with a squaring fence on the bottom. The saw's base rests against the guide's "fence."

- Place three or four 2x4s across sawhorses to support a complete sheet of 1/2-inch plywood (photo above). For each of the shelf bits, measure and mark the plywood, then cut with a circular saw and a cutting guide. The cutting guide will ensure that your cuts are completely straight and that chip-out is minimized.

- After that, stick and nail all of the pieces together (photo below). It's easier to draw pen lines on the upper and bottom panels first, so you'll know where to drive the filler nails after the top and bottom panels are covered.

- With all eight parts cut to order, putting the shelf together with glue and nails is a breeze.

- Start by placing the front rail (C) on top of your workbench (an old hollow-core door or plywood scrape on sawhorses works well), along with a couple of small support blocks cut from a 24.

- These blocks will support the top panel as you glue and nail it to the front rail. To push 1-in. brads, carefully align the top and front parts with an 18-gauge pneumatic brad nailer.

- Now glue and nail the side rails (D) to the top panel by standing them on end.

- Turn it over and use glue and brads to secure the fillers (E). The fillers should be equally spaced, but don't worry about being too precise because they'll be covered until the bottom panel is mounted (B). Nail each of the fillers through the front rail.

- Then turn the whole thing over and nail each of the fillers through the top panel. Now turn the whole piece over and nail the lower panel into fillers.

- The exposed plywood edges on the upper and bottom panels are sealed with veneer. The veneer won't stick properly if those edges aren't completely smooth and flat with the surfaces of the front and side rails.

- Using a random orbit sander and 100-grit sandpaper, sand all flush. Lay the roll flat, veneer side down, and draw a 3 in. wide straight line along the length of the roll with a marker and straightedge.

- When you add the veneer forward and sides of the rack, you'll have 1/4 in. of overhang.

- With a pair of scissors, cut the veneer strip along the line, then cut it into three sections for the front and two sides, leaving 1/4 in. of overhang on each end.

- Add the veneer to the side first, making sure the veneer is parallel to the shelf.

- Peel and stick just a few inches at a time and press the veneer in place with a block of wood. If you don't have it on completely straight the first time, cutting the bits slightly larger will help.

- Using one of the two sides of an edge-banding trimmer to trim the veneer flat with the shelf.

- When trimming with the grain of the veneer, this approach works well, but not when trimming through it. Back the veneer up with a wood block and trim the veneer flush (on the sticky side) with a sharp knife for the short cuts around the grain.

- It's also possible to use a handheld router with a flush-trimming bit. The front veneer piece should be installed after the sides.

- Then, in the back of the rack, drill some countersink holes for some No. 8 screws. The holes should be spaced about 12 inches apart and 3/4 inches from the back edge.

- Make a 1-1/2 inches x 1-3/8 inches x 70-3/4 inches wall cleat (H) out of a straight 2x4.

- Cut the plywood pieces to width with your circular saw and the same cutting guidance you used to slice the plywood pieces to width (place another 24 under the guide to prevent it from tipping).

- Cut the cleat to width before cutting it to length with a crosscut. With a little wiggle space, the narrow part of the cleat should fit into the hollow opening in the rack.

- Find and mark the stud positions on the wall with an electronic stud finder and painter's tape.

- Predrill holes in the wall cleat slightly smaller than the diameter of the lag screws' shanks after transferring the stud positions. Drill pilot holes in the wall using the cleat as a drilling aid when keeping the cleat to the wall.

- 4-inch lag screws are driven via the cleat and through the wall.
- Begin by driving a lag screw into one end of the cleat, checking for level, and then screwing the other end down before turning the middle screws.
- Place the shelf on the cleat and secure it against the wall. You'll notice some slight gaps between the shelf and the wall if your wall isn't completely smooth.
- If you don't mind the holes, you can remove them by "scribing" the shelf to match the contours of the wall.
- Drag a pencil against the wall and draw a line across the top of the shelf to scribe. The line fits the wall's contours.
- Sand up to the pencil line with a belt sander. Sanding freehand with the belt sander is difficult because if the sander is not held exactly perpendicular to the shelf, the scribe on the upper and bottom panels will not match, and the shelf will not fit tightly against the wall.
- Instead, flip the belt sander over and clamp it to a makeshift worktable, such as an old door or a scrap of plywood.
- Turn it on and change the belt tracking until the belt just disappears under the worktable's surface. Slowly sand the shelf level against your workbench until it reaches the pencil line.
- Force some "stainable" wood filler into each nail hole with your fingertip or a putty knife. Since the filler can shrink as it dries, leave a little extra in each hole—enough to protrude from the plywood.
- After it has dried, use a random orbit sander and 100- and 150-grit sandpaper to sand both sides of the rack.

- Vacuum or clean away the sawdust after sanding with the 100-grit so loose granules don't scuff the shelf as you sand with the 150-grit. Vacuum the dust or clean it away with a tack cloth before applying the stain according to the manufacturer's instructions.

- Wait a few hours before applying a second coat if you want the shelf to appear darker. After staining, wait a day or two before applying three coats of polyurethane for safety.

- Drive 1-5/8-inches screws through the pilot holes you drilled earlier and into the wall cleat while holding the shelf over the cleat and close to the wall. To keep the shelf in place while you drive the others, start with one of the middle screws.

- Coat the exposed screw heads with a "non-hardening" style of wood filler colored to match your stain until the shelf is secured.

- This form of putty remains soft, allowing you to dig it out if you ever want to remove the shelf.

Chapter 7: Outdoor Woodworking Projects

To work on one of these outdoor woodcraft ventures, you don't need to be an expert carpenter or have specialized equipment. Every one of the easy projects in this collection includes step-by-step instructions and progress tips.

1. Timber Outdoor Bench

We knew exactly what we expected from a bench, and this one delivers! Low cost, sleek design, rock-solid construction, low maintenance, and extremely simple to build.

Time: Half-day

Difficulty: Beginner

Cost: Around 100-250 dollars

Materials Required:

- Washers
- Lag screws
- 4 x 6 timbers
- Black spray paint
- Exterior stain

Instructions:

- Make a note of how long each component is. Three of the timbers will be used as bench seat "beams." When you buy the timbers, they'll be slightly longer than 8 feet, so you'll have to cut a little off either end to make them exactly 96 inches long.
- Place each piece of wood on a pair of sawhorses and sketch a pencil line on all 4 sides with a Speed Square.
- Make three cuts. Make a full-depth cut with your circular saw blade.
- Create the first cut on one of the large "backs" of the timber, using your square as a reference.
- It's unlikely that you'll be able to cut all the way through in one pass; three passes will suffice.
- When you're finished with the first cut, turn the timber on its edge, start the saw, and insert the blade partway into the (slit) you just made to align the blade for the next cut.
- Finish the second cut by guiding the saw with your square once more, then flip the timber and repeat the process for the third and final cut. Cut the remaining pieces to length in the same manner.
- Using a random orbit sander and 60-grit sandpaper, remove any saw marks that remain.

- Notches should be marked. The joinery that joins the legs to the seat beams seems complex, but it's very straightforward. L-shaped notches in the legs protect the outside beams of the bench's seat.

- The seat beams often have U-shaped notches cut into them so that the leg faces can rest about 1/4 inch above the beams.

- A circular saw, a square, and a sharp wood chisel are used to make all of the notches in the same way.

- Tip each of the outside beams on its end and mark pattern lines for the sides and bottoms of the notches with a pencil and your square. Make Xs to help you remember where to cut.

- Cut the shoulder blades. Adjust your circular saw blade to the correct depth, then make a perfectly straight cut on either side of the notch using the square as a guideline (clamp it down if necessary). Per notch, the beams receive two shoulder cuts. Each notch results in one shoulder cut on the legs.

- Between the shoulder cuts, you made for the notches in the beams, cut a sequence of freehand kerfs. Since each notch on the legs only has one shoulder cut, start the kerf cuts at the ends and work your way up to the shoulder cut.

- When you're finished carving, use your hammer's claw to remove the thin slivers of wood.

- With a sharp wood chisel, tidy the "cheek" of each notch.

- The sharp edges of the seat beams and legs can cause splinters, so take care of them now before assembling the bench. Place the beams and legs on sawhorses and use a router and a 1/4-inches round-over bit to round over all the sharp edges.

- Be sure to turn the router counterclockwise. If you don't have a router, a block plane, sanding block, or random orbit sander will suffice. The edges of the notches should not be rounded over.

- If you want to paint your bench, do so now before you put anything together. Since pressure-treated lumber is wet when you buy it, you can need to let it dry out a little before staining. Read the instructions on the can carefully.
- Fit the L-shape grooves of the legs into those U-shape notches by turning the outside beams for the seat inverted across your sawhorses with the U-shape grooves facing out.
- The tops of the legs should be level with the tops of the seat beams, and the L-shape notches should fit nicely into the U-shape notches. The fronts of the legs will protrude about 1/4 inch from the seat beams.
- If the joints won't go together by hand, use a rubber mallet or a dead blow hammer to force them together. If they still don't match, you will need to use your chisel to fine-tune the fit of each joint.
- Place the third beam (the one without grooves) between the other two beams, making sure the gaps are about 1/2 inch apart.
- Set the ledgers between the knees, bring them together tightly, and temporarily secure them with long clamps.
- Drill two pilot holes through each L-shape notch and one below each notch's shoulder (Figure A) and one hole in the middle of each ledger through the tops of the legs for lag screws.
- After that, spray-paint the lag screw and washer heads and let them dry before screwing them in.
- Start driving the screws with washers into all of the pilot holes you drilled when they're dry. A driver with a socket is ideal for this, but a wrench or ratchet will suffice. If the lag screws become scuffed, paint them again.

2. Raised Planter

Our planter is the best in terms of ease of use, durability, and convenience. It's also a lovely addition to your patio or deck, thanks to the curves and trim. You'll get approximately 8 square feet of planting space.

Time: Full day

Difficulty: Beginner

Cost: Around 100-250 dollars

Materials Required:

- treated dimensional lumber
- 5/4 decking material
- 2×4 scrap
- Three inches exterior screws
- Plywood

- 1¼-inches screws
- Soil
- landscape fabric

Tools Required:

- Saw
- Chisel
- Square
- A washer
- Sandpaper
- Clamps

Instructions:

- Chop the four legs (A) to the desired length, then mark the top and bottom grooves.
- Set the depth of your saw to 1¼-inches and develop several cuts no more than half inches apart.
- Pry the wounds with a chisel; the little fingers can shear off. With a chisel, flatten the remaining nubs. Take a 24 scrap and check to see if it would fit into the notch.
- Set the depth of your saw to Two inches and develop several cuts near the notch's edge (to create a square base).
- Extend the fingers. Make a long cut to finish the notch. Since your saw won't go all the way through the leg, you'll have to turn it over and cut it from the other hand. Notice that your grooves should be the same length as your 2x4s and 2x12s.
- Cut the box sides to length, then label the shelf supports with a rectangle, a paint can, and a washer.

- Use a circular saw for the straight cuts and a jigsaw for the curves. Using sandpaper or a router with a round-over piece, soften the cut edges.
- With three-inches exterior screws, join the side to the ends.
- Drill holes and push the screws into the wood until the heads are partially sunk. You may use exterior wood filler to cover the heads or leave them uncovered.
- Using a framing square, mark the leg positions One inch from the ends of the sides. Place the legs in place and secure them to the side with 3-inch screws.
- Mount the lower support boards by turning the planter upside down.
- These add a decorative touch to the plywood bottom while still supporting it.
- Secure the rungs in the leg notches with 3-inch screws. Screw the bottom supports in place so that they stretch about 5/8 inches inside the frame. On both sides, the bulge should be the same.
- Configure the slats for the bottom shelves and stand the planter upright. They should be about a quarter-inch apart.
- As required, cut the outer slats apart and notch the corners. Drill three or four one-inch holes.
- Drainage holes are about 1/2 inch in diameter. Start at the bottom of each end board and work your way up. Place the 3/4-inch-thick piece of wood on top of the 3/4-inch-thick piece of wood.
- Install the plywood bottom and secure it with a few 1¼-inch screws.

- Screw the shelf slats (G) into place in an even pattern. To fit around the hips, notch the end slats. After that, put the planter's bottom in place.

- The optional lattice panel trellis is a great function for those who want to grow plants that need help.

- To begin, rip a 5/46 x 10-foot board in half. Build the panel framework, then tear scrap material into 5/4 x 5/4 stops and lock them to the frame.

- Slice the lattice to size, position it in the frame, and use 3d nails to secure it to the stops. Drive screws through the panel legs into the planter box to secure the lattice panel to the back.

- The planter was given a coat of exterior stain. You could also leave your wood untreated and allow it to weather to a soft grey.

- Cover the bottom of the planter box with landscape cloth, allowing it to stretch a few inches up either side to prevent soil from seeping out the drainage holes. Start digging after filling the planter with soil or another growing medium.

- Screw the shelf supports to the shelf boards, with the inner ones extending only past the box's inside edge.

- Install the side trim, allowing the edges of the trim to stretch slightly inward as well.

3. Picnic Table

Are you looking for a unique outdoor table? This guide will teach you how to make a round Craftsman-style picnic table for your patio or backyard deck.

Time: Multiple days

Difficulty: Intermediate

Cost: Around 100-250 dollars

Materials Required:

ITEM	QUANTITY
2x4 x 8'	2
4x4 x 8'	1
1x4 x 12'	1
5/4 x 6" x 12'	3
1x8 x 8' (for clamping jig)	1
1/2" dia. x 12" drill bit	1
2" galv. deck screws	22
1-5/8" galv. deck screws	70
5/16" x 26-1/2" threaded rod	4
5/16" nuts and washers	8
Brown caulk	1 tube
Water-repellent preservative	1 qt.

Tools Required:

- Jigsaw
- Miter saw
- Hacksaw
- Straightedge
- Wood chisel
- Circular saw
- Clamps
- Orbital sander
- Rasp
- Cordless drill
- Countersink drill bit
- Square

Stuff to be cut:

Cutting List

KEY	PCS.	SIZE & DESCRIPTION
A	1	2x4 x 46"
B	1	2x4 x 26"
C	2	2x4 x 41"
D	4	4x4 x 23-7/8"
E	5	1x4 x 3-1/2"
F	2	5/4 x 6" x 30"
G	2	5/4 x 6" x 42"
H	5	5/4 x 6" x 50"
J	2	1x4 x 24"
K	4	1x4 x 18"

Instructions:

- Cut the four sections (parts A, B, and C) that make up the X-shaped feet and top support to the lengths specified on the list.
- The smoothest cuts would come from a blade made for trimming. Make a line in the center of each board.
- Place the boards on a pair of sawhorses and lock them together edge to edge, ensuring that the lines you drew earlier are all aligned.
- Draw a line through all four boards to indicate where the half-lap cutout would go. The overlap of the boards is made possible by this cutout.
- Adjust your circular saw to cut half the thickness of your boards (test with scraps), then saw a sequence of cuts to remove the wood from the half-lap cutouts.

- For greater precision, use a square to direct the saw around the cutout's outside edges. (A router with a dado bit or a table saw with a blade may also be used to make this cut.) Until removing the clamps, test the cutout with a scrap 24. With a chisel or rasp, clean up the cutout.

- Prepare the four boards for cutting the beveled ends. Since each half-lap joint is constructed with one piece upside down, you must turn one of parts A or B (not both) and one of parts Cover before cutting the beveled ends.

- Cut the angled ends by aligning the ends of the boards, clamping them together. Mark the cutting line on the ends of the boards so that when you cut, the boards support the big part of the saw base. (The bevel cuts can also be done with a miter saw.)

- Flip the boards over and sand all of the cut surfaces at the same time after the cut. Then, at the opposite end, loosen the clamps and repeat the operation.

- In sections A, B, and C, mark and drill the one-inch holes. Be sure to drill them on the sides of the boards that aren't beveled. Drill the 5/16-inch holes after that.

- Cut the four 444 bits that will be the pedestal legs into four pieces (part D). Label a line on all four sides with a circular saw and cut from opposite sides. It's more important to have flat and square ends and all four parts the same length than to have them exactly the length specified in the Cutting List. So, if you need to trim them, go ahead and do so.

- Drill a 1/2-inch hole halfway down each pedestal leg's center. Make sure the bit is parallel to the leg by carefully inspecting it. By the way, using a spade bit in an extension would burn out both your weapons and your drill.

- Sand everything you've done so far. Install a nut on the threaded rod and use a hacksaw to cut it to length. To machine, the threads, file the cut end smooth and remove the nut from it. Assemble the two base pieces (C) into an "X" and place them on sawhorses or blocks to support them. Place the 44 legs on the foundation, top them with pieces A and B, and secure the device with threaded rods. From both sides, tighten the bolts. Fix the feet in place (E). Brown caulk can fill the holes left by the nuts.

- Cut the boards F, G, and H to the lengths specified in the Cutting List to begin constructing the top. Sections F and G are cut after the longest bits (H). In the center of each board, draw a line across the back. Then, build a clamping jig out of 1/8. Place the boards on it with their center lines aligned and 1/8-inch cardboard spacers between them, upside down. Just enough to keep the boards in place, tighten the jig wedges.

- Form a circle on the boards and nail a nail in the center of the middle board. For the compass, use a cable. Remove the boards from the clamping jig, use a jigsaw to cut out the arcs, and reassemble the top, including the spacers, on the clamping jig. A wedge block would have to be moved.

- Install the inverted pedestal assembly and secure it with screws. Cut and screw down the cleat boards (J and K). Replace the spacers and sand the top of the table. After that, simply apply an exterior finish.

Chapter 8: Tips for Woodworking

Woodworking can be a lot of fun, but it can also be intimidating for newcomers. Fortunately, our editors and readers enjoy sharing their go-to advice.

- By using my belt sander, we were able to shave my pencil into a half-pencil. My changed pencil will now travel straight up along the template's edge because of the flat edge.

- As a beginner woodworker, your primary concern should be your safety. This is particularly true when working with small components.

- One of the first things a novice woodworker can discover is that the measurements of the real wood being used are not quite as they appear. The famous "two by four" board is simply 1.5" by 3.5" rather than 2" x 4".

- You don't need to use a special container if you just need to mix a small amount of epoxy for a project. Using just painter's tape, you can build a DIY mixing surface right on your workbench. All you have to do now is lay down pieces of tape overlapping each other to prevent any epoxy from getting on your bench. All you have to do now is strip off the tape and throw it away when you're finished.

- Staining- To make the job easier, you can use a regular spray bottle. Simply spray the desired area and brush away any excess with a clean rag.

- Should you need to sand down any nasty curves, a plain, everyday notepad will do the trick. To sand around curves with complicated arcs, notepads have the right amount of stiffness and versatility.

- And if you accidentally leave the top off your Elmer's wood glue and it becomes too dense to use, you can re-energize it. Simply pour in a small amount of vinegar and observe as the glue reverts to its original state.

- Do you own an old bike that you no longer use? The bike's inner tubes serve as excellent clamps for tasks with unusual angles.

Conclusion

Woodworking is the process of making things out of wood. The learning of carpentry skills, which can be used to create a career, is one of the advantages of woodworking as a hobby. Woodworking also instills patience, attentiveness, coordination, and planning skills, all of which are essential in social situations and applicable to various professions. Furthermore, learning woodworking skills will assist academically disadvantaged people in establishing a livelihood. Easy designing and measurements can also be used to improve one's math skills. It's also worth noting that woodworking requires some light but extremely beneficial body exercises. Overall, woodworking has physical, social, health, and educational advantages, and any person can, if he is persistent enough, master this art and create truly wonderous crafts.

www.ingramcontent.com/pod-product-compliance
Lightning Source LLC
Chambersburg PA
CBHW080403030726
47601CB00003B/229